COMMENTS ON THE P

'If you pick this up, and open t
you will want to read more, anc
questions put by the Philosophe
and fearless curiosity, and the ar
and in different styles: some
speculative, but all of them mar.

directness, and brevity. Some responses will make you think, or inspire you. Others might make you argue back, or disagree strongly. Either way, it will help you to work out what you think and believe, and what you don't know at all. You may find some answers. Definitely you will find better questions. It is a hugely stimulating book. It will appeal to children and teenagers, certainly, but also to anyone, of any age, who is still open to thinking curiously and non-dogmatically about the big questions in life, and about life. I know of nothing else quite like it'.

Professor Christopher Insole, Professor of Philosophical Theology and Ethics, University of Durham and Australian Catholic University

'Someone once said that we are led by the questions we ask. Petra and Thora Vardy's direct and profound questions have made for an informative and challenging book. In the answers they receive there is wisdom and insight from a variety of perspectives, which, it is hoped, will enlighten, and encourage others in their exploration of the things of faith.'

The Most Revd and Rt Hon Stephen Cottrell, Archbishop of York

'This is a book like no other, not only for the young but for everyone who wants to engage in deep thinking about life, death, the world, relationships and God. A thoroughly accessible gem that will stretch your thinking and stir your imagination.'

Dr Anna Abrams, Principal, Margaret Beaufort Institute, Cambridge

'Peter Vardy's daughters demonstrate an adventurous curiosity that opens up the world. Asking pointed questions about meaning, the responses range widely, but deeply. This is an intelligent, fascinating and challenging read.'

The Rt Revd Nick Baines, Lord Bishop of Leeds

'This excellent new book, from one of our great contemporary philosophers, shows again Peter Vardy's excellent ability to communicate complex ideas in a readily comprehendible way, to challenge thinking and to stimulate discussion and debate.

'The questions posed by Vardy's daughters, Petra and Thora, are a wonderful springboard for a journey into philosophy and theology.

They demonstrate the power of questions to bring orthodoxies into the light of examination and the responses, from a host of philosophers and theologians, can be used in a variety of ways.

'As an introduction to many of the classical arguments, they initiate the newcomer into the world of philosophy and theology. For those new to the field and the experienced, they invite response and challenge – for no position is without both merits and faults.

'This book will be an excellent resource for the classroom as the questions can be put to children of all ages to initiate discussion. As Petra and Thora demonstrate, it is often the young who can see more than those whose thinking has become settled and even ossified.

'This gadfly of a book is a most welcome addition to Vardy's outstanding publications over the years, as well as a fascinating insight into the quality of conversation around their supper table!'

Jeremy Walker, Head Master, St Peter's School, York

'Today we are in danger of forgetting that theology and philosophy are not hobbies, but existential responses to human questions that call out of our depths. Those questions have the complexity and simplicity of youthful minds, and have been voiced here with a wonderful barefaced integrity by Petra and Thora. As a collection, the responses are epiphanic not systematic, illustrative of the diverse ways the mind makes sense of this world and our place in it. Read this book and remind yourself that the big questions matter and that loyalty to the future depends on us taking them seriously.'

Dr Mark Oakley, Dean of St John's College, Cambridge, UK

'This book presents important questions everyone should be asking together with answers which combine clarity and sensitivity. As a teacher with over 20 years' experience, I consider this book ideal background reading for any GCSE or A level student of Religious Studies. Furthermore, each question could be taken as a discussion starter across any key stage. I highly recommend this engaging and fully accessible book.'

Victoria Collett, Head of Religious Studies, Malvern St James School

'There is nothing as disarming and refreshing as a couple of young people getting together and asking the big questions about life and the search for meaning. It's pleasing and rewarding when big minds with lots of experience have the humility to answer these questions in an accessible way. That's the surprising delight of *The Philosophers' Daughters*.'

Fr Frank Brennan SJ, Rector, Newman College University of Melbourne

THE PHILOSOPHERS' DAUGHTERS

THE PHILOSOPHERS' DAUGHTERS

Two young peoples' big questions answered by leading philosophers, scientists, educators and religious thinkers from around the world

Edited by PETER VARDY

Questions by PETRA AND THORA VARDY
Illustrated by DAN COHN-SHERBOK

DARTON·LONGMAN + TODD

First published in 2023 by
Darton, Longman and Todd Ltd
1 Spencer Court
140 – 142 Wandsworth High Street
London SW18 4JJ

ISBN: 978-1-915412-21-8

A catalogue record for this book is available from the British Library.

Designed and produced by Judy Linard

Printed and bound in Great Britain by Bell & Bain, Glasgow

DEDICATION

This book is dedicated to Wendy Rowe and Judy Grill

Two wonderful Godmothers to Petra and Thora who have made an enormous difference to their lives.

contents

HOW DO I MAKE SENSE OF:

Introduction

Children ask the best questions.

Schools and parents do not educate children into asking questions: they educate them into thinking within tramlines. By the time they get to adulthood, the questions children ask are often dismissed as foolish, but they are nevertheless profound.

We all tend to be educated into cultural and other frameworks. Being willing to challenge these frameworks is the path to wisdom – although many parents consider that this is to be discouraged as their own assumptions then have to be challenged.

Most profound questions do not have simple answers.

These questions arose from my wife, Charlotte's, and my daughters, Petra and Thora, up to their present ages (9 and 12). They raised these questions over the last five years and a record was kept of these. I, as a philosopher and former Vice-Principal of Heythrop College, the specialist philosophy and theology College of the University of London, have attempted to answer each. Prominent figures from many fields including top universities from the UK, USA, Australia, Ireland, Germany, Italy, New Zealand as well as senior religious figures, educators and others have attempted their own answers. Some questions have answers from several contributors. Contributors were initially given a choice of questions to answer but, inevitably, as replies came in, the choices became more restricted.

Reponses were requested to be not longer than 500 words and to be accessible to an intelligent teenager. A few answers did not meet the latter criteria – the editor has sometimes inserted in italics and between square brackets [ ] his own understanding of some terms to help the reader, but these are brief and were not included in the contributors' answers. A few, rare, answers did not address the question. We are, nevertheless, very grateful to all those who did respond and for their considerable efforts. We tried to get responses from some prominent atheists and humanists on religious issues but without great success. 'The Philosopher's reply' to each question is provided by the editor.

Some of the questions that Petra and Thora came up with were the result of being taught at home during Covid lockdown. They explored something of the nature of different dimensions through watching films like *Flatland* and discussed a little of the nature of quantum reality and the singularity. They examined the basic nature of DNA and the ethical challenges our increased knowledge represents. They also watched the news regularly and discussed matters that arose. The girls attended a local Cathedral where they were often bored and constantly raised questions about what Jesus said in the Gospels and what went on in the Cathedral. They were and are compassionate and concerned about those who had to choose between feeding their children or heating their home as well as the plight of refugees and the homeless, whilst others were concerned with new cars and fashion labels. They constantly came back to questions about the point of existence and what it meant to be human. They recognised the reality of relationship breakdowns and suffering and all these gave rise to more questions. What has become clear in preparing this book and communicating with contributors and others is that many other children have remarkably similar questions.

Without the illustrations of Dan Cohn-Sherbok, this book would have been greatly the poorer. We are grateful to David Moloney and to Darton, Longman and Todd for being willing to publish this book as well as to Wendy Rowe and Moira Siara for their invaluable help.

Dr Peter Vardy, Editor
Bracken Ridge Farm, North Yorkshire
June 2022

LIST OF Contributors

Dr Anna Abram (Margaret Beaufort Institute, University of Cambridge)

The Rt Revd Nick Baines (Lord Bishop of Leeds)

Professor Michael Barnes SJ (Marquette University)

Professor Gwen Bellamy (School of Mathematics and Statistics, University of Glasgow)

Professor Frank Brennan SJ (Human Rights Lawyer and Academic)

Rt Revd Peter Carnley AC (former Primate of the Anglican Church of Australia)

Rabbi Professor Dan Cohn-Sherbok (University of Wales)

Br. Guy Consolmagno SJ (Director, Vatican Observatory)

The Most Reverend and Right Honourable Stephen Cottrell (Archbishop of York)

Professor Gavin D'Costa (University of Bristol)

Cardinal John Dew, (Archbishop of Wellington, New Zealand)

Professor Robin Dunbar (Anthropologist and Evolutionary Psychologist, University of Oxford)

Professor C. Stephen Evans (Baylor University)

David Garratt (former Principal Daramalan College, Canberra)

Dr Gabrielle Gionti SJ (Italian National Institute for Nuclear Physics)

The Revd Christopher Gleeson SJ (former Head of Riverview College, Sydney)

Assistant Professor Zohar Hadromi-Allouche (Trinity College, Dublin)

Frances Horner (Lawyer, Washington DC)

Professor Christopher Insole (University of Durham)

Dr Peter Jones (Quaker & Retired Teacher, Tasmania)

The Right Reverend John Keenan (Bishop of Paisley)

Fr Dr Richard Leonard SJ (Parish Priest, North Sydney)

Dr Tommy Lynch (University of Chichester)

Dr Tim MacNaught (Former Head of Religious Studies, Anglican Grammar Schools, Melbourne)

Professor Tom McLeish (University of York)

Canon the Lady Ailsa Newby (Ripon Cathedral)

Dr Louise Nelstrop (Margaret Beaufort Institute, University of Cambridge)

Cardinal Vincent Nichols, (Archbishop of Westminster)

Professor Aileen O'Donoghue (Department of Physics, St. Lawrence University)

Canon Dr Mark Oakley (Dean, St John's College, University of Cambridge)

Cardinal George Pell, (Australia)

Dr Sue Price (Margaret Beaufort Institute, University of Cambridge)

Revd Dr Rainer Hagencord (Director of the Institute for Theological Zoology, Munster)

James Roose-Evans (Theatrical Director)

Sr Dr Gemma Simmonds CJ, (Director of Religious Life Institute, Cambridge)

Professor Stefan Sorgner, John Cabot University, Rome

The Right Revd Rachel Treweek (Bishop of Gloucester)

Charlotte Vardy (Teacher and Author)

Grace Akosua Williams (Social Entrepreneur & Lawyer, Tasmania)

Gerard Windsor (Author and Literary Critic)

The Rt Hon. The Lord Wallace of Tankerness KC (Moderator, Church of Scotland)

Catrina Young (Deputy Head, Dixie Grammar School)

HOW DO I MAKE SENSE OF THE UNIVERSE AND THE NATURAL WORLD?

SCIENCE CANNOT EXPLAIN HOW
SOMETHING COMES FROM NOTHING...
AND THAT'S CERTAINLY SOMETHING!

1.

'What caused the Big Bang?'

THE PHILOSOPHER'S REPLY:

Almost every scientist since the 1950s agrees that the universe began with a singularity (the initial explosion which arose from no prior state of affairs and which caused the existence of the universe) about 13.8 billion years ago. The discovery of background radiation (radiation left over from the initial explosion) and the rate of expansion of the universe point to this being the case. Before the singularity there was no time and space: these came into existence with the singularity. The problem is to explain the singularity.

One of the reasons that Professor Fred Hoyle, a lifelong atheist, for so long rejected the idea that the universe had a beginning is that science cannot explain how something can come from nothing – the very idea offends against one of the basic principles of science. In the last seventy years explaining the singularity has become much harder. We now know that the conditions of the singularity had to be incredibly, unbelievably precise. If any one of the large number of variables had been different by the tiniest fraction there would have been no universe, no stars, no planets and no you or me. The problem is how to explain this extraordinary improbability.

Professor Richard Swinburne of Oxford University likens the chance of the singularity's conditions being absolutely right

19

to create stars, planets and eventually life to the following example. Imagine ten machines that automatically randomly shuffle packs of card. Machines such as these are in common use in casinos across the world. The odds of one pack of cards being randomly shuffled and producing a particular card is 52 to 1. Now imagine two packs of cards being randomly shuffled at the same time. The odds of both packs of cards both coming up with identical cards is 52 x 52 to 1. Now imagine all ten packs of cards being shuffled, The odds of every one of the packs of cards all coming up with the same card is 52 to the power of 10 – 1.44555105949057e+17 to 1. These are about the same odds of the singularity having precisely the right conditions.

There are only three alternatives that I know of to explain this improbability.

1. To say, 'it just happened' and we don't know how. Almost no scientist would accept this explanation as it is not an explanation at all.
2. To posit God or an Intelligence that created the universe
3. To argue that the improbability is so high that we must live in a multiverse. An incredibly advanced civilisation with access to unbelievable computing power produced a near infinite number of possible initial conditions and we happen to be in the one that was right for stars and carbon-based life forms to develop. We are living, effectively, in a virtual world, a hologram. This is a serious possibility adopted by an increasing number of scientists.

Professor Sir John Polkinghorne, one of the world's most eminent scientists, came to religious faith late in life because he came to the conclusion that the second of the above hypotheses made more sense of the evidence than any alternative. There is, of course, no evidence in favour of the third alternative and Polkinghorne argued it was a desperate attempt by those who wished to avoid the second. It also requires an explanation for the existence of the very advanced civilisation that is suggested to exist.

DAVID GARRATT

Writer and former Principal, Daramalan College, Canberra ACT, Australia

This is a question that has long challenged me too. The existence of a 'singularity' capable of expanding into a universe is really incomprehensible to me, especially since that universe currently just keeps expanding. Matter must still be bursting into existence. It is surely not possible for it all to have existed in the 'singularity'. How did the singularity happen? And what caused the singularity to suddenly 'explode'? I really have no idea. For people of faith the answer is fairly simple. Assuming they believe in the 'Big Bang' explanation of how the universe started, for them it is God who caused the singularity to exist and God who triggered the Big Bang. To satisfy my view that the singularity could not possibly have contained all that is in the still growing universe, it would be God again who brings the extra matter into existence. That is a comfortable answer if you are a believer. A person who does not believe in God is left with the cause just being how things are. But how did nature come to exist? If I conclude that it had to be created by God, then the next mystery I have is how did God come to be? So, however I try to answer the question I am left with a mystery. The existence of a God or the existence of an astounding nature are equally challenging propositions.

Dr Gabrielle Gionti SJ

Italian National Institute for Nuclear Physics

The Big Bang theory is the most successful theory for describing the beginning of our Universe, the Universe in which we live. Recent measurements, made by the Planck satellite, confirm that the Universe started to expand 13.82 billion years ago and, since then, continues to expand. One has to imagine, in analogy, the Universe as the two-dimensional surface of a balloon. The Galaxies, which populate the Universe, stay on the surface of this balloon. As long as the balloon expands the distances among the Galaxies increase. This is the universe expansion.

If this universe expands now, going back in time the universe was smaller and smaller until it reached a time in which the universe should have been small as a 'point'. This is the 'Big Bang'. The first person to think about it was the famous Belgian cosmologist and priest, Monsignor George Lemaître. It is a hot and dense phase of the Universe. Some people think that the universe started with an explosion, but this is truly a metaphor. We do not really know if this was true or not, certainly there was an initial phase of the universe so hot and dense that particles did not exist. There was only radiation.

The Big Bang or beginning of the universe has fostered, in the past, some attempts to connect the Big Bang theory with the creation histories in the beginning of the book of Genesis in the Bible. It circulated the 'wrong' ideas that Big Bang theory seemed to confirm the doctrine of creation we read in the Bible. The 'Let there be light' (*Fiat Lux* in Latin) is the explanation of the beginning of the Universe in the sense that God created the Universe (the Universe emerged from the 'hands of God'), which immediately expanded. This way of thinking is called 'concordism' and really does not work. It was an attempt to merge scientific theories with theological doctrines.

We do not know in science the cause of the Big Bang, why the Universe started to expand. We do not know who created the initial energy of the Universe, when it was small like a point. Thinking of God as the creator of the initial energy of the Universe, a cause of it, and the cause of its expansion is believing in the idea of 'God of the Gaps'. That is a concept of God that one introduces when one cannot explain something using science. It is, substantially, a bad concept of God. This God is more like the Greek God than the Christian God. It is a very human way of describing God. Surely it is not the God revealed by Jesus Christ, which is, mainly, The God of Love.

Today we have theories, like pre-Big Bang theory, which claim that there was a 'time' before the beginning of the Universe. In this 'time', the Universe already existed in some state. It had a particular behaviour and from it the Universe we know originated and expanded: hence the Pre-Big Bang theory answer to the question about the cause of the Big Bang. These are only theoretical speculations and there are not yet experimental data to confirm or disprove them. Therefore, one can understand the danger of thinking of God as the Creator of our Universe at the Big Bang. In fact, if the theory of pre-Big Bang is shown to be true in the future, then we do not need the concept of God to explain the Big Bang. Then this could imply that God's existence is not needed.

2.

'Assuming the Big Bang occurred, how did it eventually create such complex human beings as we are?'

THE PHILOSOPHER'S REPLY:

The 'Big Bang' or singularity was an almost uniformly expanding ball of energy. The laws of nature, which science itself does not explain but which it uses as a basis for explanation, were present from the initial moment. The very early universe produced hydrogen and helium which have a fairly boring chemistry. There was no carbon in this initial stage. There is only one place where carbon is made and that is in the nuclear furnaces at the heart of stars. We human beings are, literally, star dust.

To create stars, however, the conditions had to be unbelievably precise as otherwise the initial gases would simply have dispersed or collapsed in on themselves and in neither case would stars have been formed. All the heavier elements necessary for life, particularly carbon, are created in stars. In the mid-1970s, the Australian physicist Brandon Carter pointed out that our universe seems particularly fine-tuned for the emergence of life. For example, if the nuclear force holding the centres of atoms together were a little weaker, then the complex atoms needed for life could never form. If it were a little stronger, all of the hydrogen in the infant universe would have fused to become helium. The precision of the singularity was partly discovered by Professor Fred Hoyle who was a lifelong atheist but when he saw the precise conditions said, 'Something must have being going on'. He refused to name this something as 'God' but suggested a cosmic Intelligence (with a capital 'I') had 'monkeyed with the laws of nature'.

Darwin's theory of natural selection argues that human beings have evolved from primitive life forms by natural selection, the survival of the fittest. The evidence in favour of natural selection is exceptionally strong – although it is not yet conclusive. There are gaps in the fossil record and there are still things that natural selection cannot explain including consciousness and human freedom (if this exists which is, of course, debatable). It is important to be clear – there is no purpose behind natural selection. It is simply survival of the fittest organisms to pass on their genes in the conditions available. As the atheist biologist Richard Dawkins puts it: *'Evolution has no long term goal. There is no long-distance target, no final perfection to serve as a criterion for selection ... The criteria for selection is always short term, either simply survival or, more generally, reproductive success... The 'watchmaker' that is cumulative natural selection is blind to the future and has no long-term goal.'*

In the last 20 years, a new branch of Darwinian natural selection has developed – this is called evolutionary psychology which is a branch of sociobiology *[a combination of biology and sociology]*. This holds that just as the physical make up of organisms evolve, so animal and human behavioural traits evolve by natural selection. This is, again, a purely biological process to ensure survival. However it is not as simple as that.

Prior to Darwin there was another largely ignored

figure. The French biologist Jean-Baptiste Lamarck (1744–1829) argued for 'soft inheritance' as the main factor driving adaptation. Lamarckism (or Lamarckian inheritance) is the claim that characteristics acquired during a lifetime can be passed onto their descendants. Darwinists reject this, but we now know that Lamarck was right. Human behaviour can affect genes. There are various examples – as but one instance, Japanese scientists inflicted pain on mice and at the same time released a perfume into their cages. They came to associate the perfume with pain. The female mice then had babies which were taken away at birth and the babies inherited the fear of the perfume even though no pain was inflicted. As another example, in 1944, the Allies launched 'Operation Market Garden' to drive the Germans back beyond the Rhine. They failed. In retaliation for Dutch assistance, tens of thousands of the Dutch were blockaded and starved for a whole winter. They had to live on 570 calories a day. Thousands of babies died and the children were stunted and, as adults, were much shorter than normal. This short stature was passed onto their children. These and other studies gives rise to 'epigenetics'. Natural selection, by itself, cannot therefore explain the world as we now know it.

We do not yet begin to understand what it means to be human at the most basic level. The one thing that is clear is that the conditions for human beings to exist at all had to be unbelievably, unimaginably precise and religious people will, not unreasonably, claim that this was no accident.

Professor Tom McLeish FRS

Professor of Natural Philosophy in the Department of Physics, University of York

A great question. It turns out that matter, and its interactions that we discover with physics and chemistry, has an astonishing property of 'self-assembly' that seems to be able to give rise to very high degrees of order in a very few places in the universe, while most of the rest of the place is very disordered. The reasons for this are mysterious, because most alternative universes that physicists have explored with mathematics, with different electric force strengths, or slightly different gravity, for example, do not generally seem to have this property. The universe needs to have properties very close indeed to the ones that it actually does have in order for very complex molecules, let alone life, to evolve in it. (I should be clear - we don't yet know how life got started, but we can guess that you do at least need a universe able to make complex molecules for this to happen).

Dr Gabrielle Gionti SJ

Italian National Institute for Nuclear Physics

This question refers to the problem of life in the Universe and, more specifically, why and how the Big Bang caused the emergence of Intelligent life on Earth. These points are closely related to two main arguments that are called the fine-tuning argument and the Anthropic Principle.

'Fine-tuning' is the recognition that all the fundamental physical constants and laws seem to be fine-tuned. If they had small different numerical values life on Planet Earth would have never emerged and our Universe would have never been fertile for life. Frankly speaking, science has not explained yet why this fine-tuning exists.

In order to answer to this question, scientists have elaborated a principle, which is quite often debated, called the 'Anthropic Principle'. There are two versions of this principle: the strong anthropic principle and the weak anthropic principle. The strong anthropic principle says that the fundamental constants of physics are fine-tuned in such a way they will necessarily allow the emergence of life on the planet Earth as well as all other Earth-like planets. This statement seems problematic as the scientific method assumes that the laws of nature are not organized, in general, in such a way to realize a specific purpose

A weaker version of the Anthropic principle is called the 'weak Anthropic principle'. This states that we can observe life from 'privileged' positions where intelligent life has emerged (since we, as living beings, are the 'observers'). We can study how the physical laws might vary in order that life could emerge on Earth or Earth-like planets. In other words, a scientist tries to vary the physical constants and also the physical laws to find if there exists some more fundamental principle or law capable to explain the fine-tuning introduced above.

Different values of the physical constants could imply the existence of many universes. Each of them has its physical laws characterised by a given numerical set of these physical constants. Some of them are favourable for the emergence of life and some are not. This has been one of the reasons for the development of the theory of multiverses. These are, in science, only early stage attempts to explain the emergence of life in our Universe. Why there is such a complex being like the human being is still an open question not completely answered.

As I said, we are sure that the physics of our universe is tuned for life on Earth and Earth-like planets. Once life has emerged on Earth, it has evolved through the mechanism of biological Evolution. Biological Evolution is based on 'mutations' happening on living beings. These mutations are, for example, variations of an organ in a certain specie which makes it fitter to survive. These mutations evolve through the mechanism of natural selection. Mutations and natural selections originate all different living beings through a process of chance (probability) and necessity (deterministic processes). The human being is the final product of all these processes. This mechanism does not assure that this path is the only possible one. The fact we have evolved along a chain up to our situation, does not ensure that if, hypothetically, we repeat the process the same thing could happen.

3.

*⁶As humans are meant
to have evolved by natural selection
through survival of the fittest, surely
morality should just be about helping
the fittest to survive? Why care for
the weak and vulnerable if survival
is all that matters?⁹*

THE PHILOSOPHER'S REPLY:

The logic of your question makes great sense. The natural world is held to have evolved by natural selection and Darwin's theory of 'the survival of the fittest' is persuasive. Yet humans care for the weak and vulnerable and allow some people to have children who, it could be argued, do not have the best genetic material from a Darwinian perspective. If survival is all that matters, then why should not human beings follow this through to its logical conclusion as you suggest? There is, however, a deep human repugnance to take such an approach and perhaps this points to the fact that 'survival of the fittest' is not a proper basis for ethics nor, indeed, the best explanation of the fullness of what it means to be human. Yes, we are advanced animals, but perhaps we are more than this. Our sense of morality points to this 'more'.

In the Superman film, *Man of Steel*, one woman from the planet Krypton, who Superman is fighting, says to him: ' you are weak ... the fact that you possess a sense of morality and we do not, gives us an evolutionary advantage. And if history has proven anything, it is that evolution always wins.' Her point is that a sense of morality can be seen as a weakness as this gets in the way of the fittest surviving. The woman is saying that because she has no sense of morality, she is in a stronger position than Superman as protection of the weak and vulnerable means that this protection renders human beings weaker than a species solely concerned with power and success. However, human beings down the ages have always maintained that survival of the fittest does not have the last word. Standing up for what is right, just and good may indeed go against passing on the 'best' genes, but some things matter more than survival. It is clear from history that however powerful, lacking in compassion and morality some leaders and the people who follow them may be, good will always triumph over evil – although it may take a long time to do so!

Professor Aileen A. O'Donoghue

Henry Priest Professor of Physics, St Lawrence University, New York, USA

We did evolve through natural selection, but it is more complicated than the phrase, 'survival of the fittest'. Survival and successful reproduction of a species requires more than physical fitness, it requires community fitness where each individual supports the community and is supported by the community. Though the weak and vulnerable may seem to have no contributions to community, if we look more closely, their very dependence is actually a contribution.

If every individual were able to survive on his or her own and was expected to provide for all their own needs, there would be little reason to develop community and we could all live individually, like bears, foxes, or other mostly solitary animals. These animals do form family groups, but the young grow to adulthood so quickly that the individual mothers are able to support them to adulthood.

Humans, however, are born so weak and vulnerable that it takes even the very fittest many years, at least the better part of two decades, to develop into self-sufficient adults. Those with direct care for the young need others in the community, who will benefit from children's contributions as adults, to support them while they support the children. This extends the network of need and contribution throughout the group. Those out acquiring resources need others to care for their young just as much as the children and their caregivers need the resources. Thus, all of us require community (family, extended family, and tribes) to help us survive and grow.

The interdependence *[the idea that members of a community depend on each other for the success of the community]* that developed among families, tribes, and larger communities expands 'fittest' to mean the community that best supports all the members as they make their individual contributions. The interdependence creates bonds and, it turns out, humans need these bonds nearly as much as we need the physical resources. This is why we're willing to extend resources to those among us who can contribute only minimally, with their need, and their love. That we do support the weakest assures all of us, even the greatest contributors among us, that we have value to the community beyond our contributions. This strengthens everyone within the community and, thus, strengthens the community. It's this strength that makes it more likely to, not just survive, but thrive than it would be if it were only willing to support contributors.

4.

‘Why do people want to go
to Mars and spend so much
money with rockets which
damage the planet when we
have a lovely planet here if we
could only fix it? Surely this
would be easier than
fixing Mars?’

THE PHILOSOPHER'S REPLY:

There are two answers to this question, and they are both right.
Some forms of space exploration are incredibly important.
They enable us to make discoveries that would otherwise be
impossible and these discoveries have transformed human
lives. New materials have been discovered, new insights
provided into our planet, new ways of monitoring what is
happening in times of climate change, the build-up of arms,
famines, locusts spreading across continents, sea level rises,
agricultural developments and many, many other areas. None
of these discoveries or new sources of information would be
possible without space exploration and the use of rockets.
We believe that the dinosaurs were destroyed by an asteroid
or comet hitting the earth and we are developing technology

to be able to intercept any such a space visitor in the future before it destroys the planet.

There is, however, another side to this. Incredibly rich billionaires such as Bezos (the head of Amazon), Branson (the head of the Virgin group of companies) and others are developing space tourism which sends millionaires into space to have an adventure. The cost of the 'ride' (which sometimes provides about thirty minutes of weightlessness) can be upwards of $250 million. There is little scientific purpose for these trips and by any standard it seems wasteful, damaging to the environment and wrong.

Which of the two above categories trips to Mars fits into is not clear. We will certainly learn a tremendous amount about the planet and our knowledge of the solar system will be increased immeasurably. Whether this is 'worth it' in terms of the cost, pollution, etc. is a debatable issue. Elon Musk seeks to colonise Mars so that, if the earth is destroyed or becomes uninhabitable, the human race could survive. It would be preferable to avoid this happening, although, being realistic, it could be argued that given the human propensity for greed and violence there may be no better chance on Mars than on earth. But that is, perhaps, too depressing!

As always there are some cases in the middle. Elon Musk has developed a reusable rocket which is now NASA's main way of re-supplying the International Space Station. He has, however, also launched thousands of tiny satellites into orbit supposedly to provide internet access across the globe but these have the side effect of creating a massive amount of space junk. Nevertheless these same satellites may provide low-cost internet access to the poorest countries on earth.

What is more complex is the huge amount being spent by the USA, China and Russia on space weapons. Space is increasingly becoming weaponised – but that is another issue!

BROTHER GUY CONSOLMAGNO SJ

Director of the Vatican Observatory and President of the Vatican Observatory Foundation

Let me start with the answer you probably expect, but then I'll turn it on its head. It is certainly true that we need to get off our planet and see it from a different perspective, a global perspective, in order to understand it well enough to 'fix' it.

For example, we know about how carbon dioxide heats up the atmosphere and surface of Earth because we have been able to study what it has done to the atmosphere and surface of Venus. So, there is a certain utility for going into space and studying other planets.

But that's not actually the reason we do it. Look at your question again, especially the part of the question that you have left unexamined. Why do people want to go to Mars? You're right; at a certain level it seems to make no sense. It won't make you rich or powerful. And yet, we want to. People want to. Why?

Many years ago, when I was a young astronomer working on projects paid for by NASA, I had exactly those doubts. Why study other planets when people are starving on this planet? So, I quit my astronomy job and went off to work with a volunteer group, the US Peace Corps, in Africa. I was assigned to teach at the University of Nairobi, a job not all that different from what I had been doing before I went to Africa. That felt disappointing to me. Every weekend I went away from Nairobi; I would travel up-country to visit my fellow volunteers who were in more remote parts of the country, where the people were poor and isolated.

But a funny thing happened when I visited them. When people heard that I was an astronomer, they wanted to hear about the latest results from the NASA missions to the planets.

They wanted to look through my little telescope at the Moon and Jupiter and Saturn. They wanted to hear about, and be a part of, the great adventure of studying the universe that was going on, and continues to go on, in the rest of the world.

Yes, they were hungry. But their minds and imaginations and souls were also hungry. All their parts that make them more than just hungry animals, the things that make them human, also needed to be fed. We do not live by bread alone.

To say 'no' to that urge to explore and understand, is to say 'no' to something essential in our humanity. Of course, we need to do all the other things that will keep our planet safe and whole. But recall the biblical story of creation … the ultimate day of creation, the seventh day, the day of rest, is when we are given the time to contemplate and appreciate the work of our Creator. The Sabbath was made for us. We were made to be astronomers!

THE RT REVD NICK BAINES
Lord Bishop of Leeds

Every development we now take for granted – modern dentistry, cars, central heating, the internet, vaccines, for example – have happened because human beings are basically curious. We seem to have a natural desire and impulse to push boundaries, to learn more, to explore possibilities. Of course, this curiosity sometimes leads to some very bad things such as nuclear weapons or climate change. But, people seem to be made to want more and know more and understand more.

This should not be a surprise. Back at the beginning of the Book of Genesis, the wonderful poem about creation has God saying, 'let there be …'. Contrary to what many people assume, what we call the 'creation narratives' don't address the question

'How did the cosmos come into being?', but, rather, 'Why is the cosmos there and what does it all mean?'. It is important not to confuse these two questions. However, as scientists and technologists pursue the 'how' questions, it is vital that poets, philosophers and theologians ask the 'why' questions.

This Genesis narrative goes on to say something vital about human beings: we are created to breed more human beings and to 'cultivate' the earth – which can be understood to include agriculture, technology, the arts and humanities ... and the sort of deep questions you are asking about why things are the way they are, and why it matters anyway.

This perhaps suggests why some people want to push every boundary, to explore where we have not gone before. Yes, some will want to go to Mars in order to see what we can get from it – minerals, resources, and so on. In other words, their motives will be economic or commercial. Most people, though, are just curious to know what Mars is about and what we might learn about the universe from it.

Mars doesn't need to be fixed. Earth does. You are right to suggest that we must not explore the unknown at the expense of putting right what is wrong here. All of us are responsible for the earth first. And the earth is, indeed, very beautiful.

5.

> **'**What is real? I'm not sure
> I know. They used to say
> photographs cannot lie but that
> is wrong. Is reality just what we
> see around us?**'**

THE PHILOSOPHER'S REPLY:

Children really do ask the best questions! Few adults would consider such a question or would dismiss it as absurd. 'How childish' they might say, 'reality is what we see around us every day.' The only thing that is very clear is that it is this response that is childish and not the question.

Until the end of the nineteenth century this response might have been considered reasonable by many scientists. This was a world dominated by Newtonian science. The atom was the fundamental, indivisible element underlying all matter. The universe was like a great clockwork machine. Light travelled in straight lines albeit at unbelievable speeds. Even before the nineteenth century, however, there were dissenting voices. Plato, the great Greek philosopher, argued that we are in a prison confined by our senses and what we take to be real are only the flickering shadows of true reality. We need to use reason to break free of our prison and to understand the ultimate timeless and spaceless nature of what is truly real. Religious people have always maintained that our present reality is only part of a much great spiritual reality which can be glimpsed in this life and poets have sought to point beyond the world of the everyday to transcendent meaning.

Since the early years of the twentieth century, scientists such as Einstein, Bohr, Schrödinger and others have uncovered something of the nature of quantum reality. The atom is certainly not indivisible and as it became possible to probe further into the nature of the reality we see around us it became more and more clear that the universe is strange, bizarre and incredibly difficult to understand. First came the discovery of electrons and then a whole range of more complex particles such as Leptons and Quarks. Light does not travel in straight lines but can be bent by gravity. There is no cosmic 'now' since time and space are intimately related. Time slows down the faster we travel. At the quantum level all the normal Newtonian laws break down. The floor you are standing on is only solid from your point of view – at the most basic level of reality there is no matter at all. Some particles can travel straight through the earth without being affected in any way. Reality, in other words, depends on our human perspective.

The great German philosopher Immanuel Kant recognised this when he argued for the distinction between the phenomenal world (the world as we experience it through our five senses) and the noumenal world (the world as it really is independent of the way it appears to us) [c.f. Question 6]. We now know this is the case since what is real is certainly far, far more complex than what we see around us and may, indeed, be a mystery.

So, the only answer I could give to your question is 'I have no idea what ultimate reality is'. Some scientists would have a much better idea than I (since I am only a philosopher) but I suspect most of them would be quick to recognise that even our present understanding of reality is, at best, only very partial. As Shakespeare's Hamlet said, 'There are more things in heaven and earth, Horatio, than are dreamt of in your philosophy.' Being willing to live with an understanding of how partial and incomplete our knowledge of reality is, may be the first step to wisdom.

Socrates considered that he was the wisest man in Athens as he really knew nothing. He set out to show people who were sure how much they knew how wrong they were. Naturally this made him very unpopular, and he was put to death for 'corrupting young people' by getting them to question the supposed 'wisdom' of their elders. Being willing to recognise how little we know is, perhaps, the path to wisdom.

Professor Tom McLeish FRS
Professor of Natural Philosophy in the Department of Physics, University of York

We don't honestly know what is real. Science can't tell us for sure what is real - we only build a picture of what the universe is around us from what we can observe and experiment on. You are right that photographs can be 'faked', but does that mean what we think is our best guess (as far as we can understand it) is 'faked'? Well it might be - but then that just makes our picture of reality bigger as our knowledge increases, Because we now have evidence that reality was larger than our first understanding of reality. Is that second, larger reality (including the faking bits of the first reality we once thought was everything) real? Or faked? The same thing happens. So there is a certain amount of faith required in our models of the universe, that they really do correspond to something real, as far as we can understand it.

6.

‘I used to love rainbows. They seemed full of mystery. Then my teacher explained they are just sunlight passing through rain and they can be explained away by science. I feel I have lost something but I am not sure what?’

THE PHILOSOPHER'S REPLY:

The great Greek philosopher, Plato, argued that beauty is not relative to culture. Beauty, like Truth, Justice and Goodness are absolute values which exist independent of human beings. They are absolute as they do not depend on peoples' opinion or on culture. Many today reject this and say that 'beauty is in the eye of the beholder' and there is certainly some truth in this. The beauty, for instance, of women is considered to vary between cultures as does what may be considered 'handsome' or good looking in men. But this is only part of the story.

C. S. Lewis gives an example of two people looking at a waterfall. One says, 'It's pretty', the other says 'It's sublime'. This is not just a matter of a difference of opinion – they are differing at a far more profound level. The person who says that the waterfall is sublime is saying that the beauty of the waterfall is not just a matter of the way some humans see things: Beauty points to a transcendent, an absolute order. The beauty can be glimpsed in the beauty of the natural world or, indeed, in many places.

Just occasionally a great mathematician will say of a particularly brilliant mathematical proof 'It's beautiful'. This is not simply a difference of opinion – they are expressing a profound commitment that mathematics, at its best, is indeed beautiful and reflects the underlying structure and order of the universe. Mathematics underpins almost all of reality from the human body to the way plants grow, from the way fir cones and sunflowers are formed to the behaviour of cyclones. The best mathematicians are sometimes in awe of the beauty they find in mathematics, and this underpins the beauty many perceptive people find in nature.

The idea, therefore, that rainbows are beautiful in no way

undermines the fact that their colours are due to refracted light – but just makes a commitment to the fact that they are far more than this. They show us a glimpse of the underlying structure of the universe, which is wonderous, incredible and, indeed, beautiful and once we lose this 'childish' insight, we lose something incredibly precious. Science matters – it matters a very great deal – but to consider that science and a material understanding of reality can provide a complete picture is a tragic mistake, albeit one that in our present culture is increasingly widespread.

CARDINAL JOHN DEW
Archbishop of Wellington, New Zealand

I understand your love for rainbows. It is not just the colours, it is the way a rainbow can appear so unexpectedly, and often after a gloomy period of weather. A rainbow seems like a pathway to another place, where there is colour and brightness and perhaps even a pot of gold …

Something which is both beautiful and mysterious touches the spiritual dimension in us which is often buried by the activities and distractions of our daily lives. When you saw a rainbow, your imagination was able to expand with ideas about what lay in behind, and beyond the rainbow, and much more. You were exploring the mysterious, and that expansion of our imagination is very good for our souls.

The explanation that the rainbow is just sunlight passing through rain is very limiting. It does nothing to draw your imagination into the mysterious. In fact, it seems to limit your imagination by providing an explanation which dismisses the mysterious. Losing the mysterious to a scientific explanation may make you feel a little sad. But there is a way out of this deflated space. If you explore how the rain affects the sunlight you will find an intricate and beautiful answer in the science. Once you understand light as the scientist knows it, how it produces colours and interacts with water to produce a rainbow, you will find joy and wonder in the rainbow again, but in a different way.

Many scientists, some of the best scientists, have a deep sense of wonder in their work as they go further into the complexities of the universe. One of the most famous scientists, Albert Einstein, knew the importance of this sense of wonder when he wrote: 'The most beautiful thing we can experience is the mysterious. It is the source of all true art and science.'

In his document *Laudato Si'* Pope Francis wrote about St Francis of Assisi who 'invites us to see nature as a magnificent book in which God speaks to us and grants us a glimpse of his infinite beauty and goodness' (*LS* 12). St Francis knew that a sense of wonder could take us to a very deep spiritual place. Take the words which disappointed you about a rainbow being 'just sunlight passing through the rain' and ask questions: 'How does this happen?' and 'What is light?' and other questions which occur to you. Go looking for the answers. You will find the joy and excitement and wonder of rainbows again.

Don't ever accept that a rainbow is just 'sunlight passing through rain'.

Brother Guy Consolmagno SJ

Director of the Vatican Observatory and President of the Vatican Observatory Foundation

There is only one word wrong in that description: the word 'just'. A rainbow is not 'just' sunlight and raindrops and physics … it is an amazing and breathtakingly beautiful bit of physics.

The maths involved are as beautiful and mysterious as the rainbow itself!

At the heart of the physics explaining how rainbows work are something called 'Maxwell's Equations'. James Clerk Maxwell was a wonderful Scottish physicist who, for my money, is up there with Einstein and Newton in the pantheon of physics greats. He was the first to assemble all the bits that other people had worked out about electricity and magnetism, write down the equations that described how they work, intuit a missing piece that no one had seen before, and then …

Well, it's not easy to explain here without university-level mathematics, but let's just say that he could read those equations like you might be able to read a poem, and he saw that they contained the explanation for how light works. Who had ever thought that light would be connected with electricity and magnetism? But as he showed, they are. One of the wonderful things about Maxwell's equations is that they are just four lines of letters and numbers that are almost, but not quite, the same form over and over; but one of them has just one tiny difference, a minus sign, which makes all the difference.

I remember one time teaching university physics when I presented these equations to my class, and the smartest student in the class (who of course was sitting in the front row) took a look at those equations and exclaimed out loud, 'Oh my God! It's a wave!'

Yes, it's a wave. That one little negative sign means that the equations can be blended together in such a way that they don't just cancel each other out, but instead become the equation for a wave. And that's how we know that electricity and magnetism can be blended into a wave, waves that we recognize now as radio waves, x-rays, microwaves … and light waves. The light waves that droplets of water can split into a rainbow.

In fact, that insight led to the invention of radio and

television, to all the electronics that go into your cell phones and computers, to the science that allows astronomers to measure the composition and temperature of distant stars … And eventually it inspired the invention of all of modern physics, from lasers to black holes. And how rainbows work.

It makes sense that the underlying physics of the universe is logical; the world wouldn't work, otherwise. But it is startling that this physics is also beautiful. It is poetry, musical counterpoint, a painting that almost but not quite repeats itself in a hypnotizing way. It is surprising, beautiful, fruitful, inspiring. It is the work of a master Artist.

Gerard Windsor
Author and literary critic

> My heart leaps up when I behold
> A Rainbow in the sky:
> So was it when my life began;
> So is it now I am a Man.
> So be it when I shall grow old,
> Or let me die!
> The Child is Father of the Man;
> And I could wish my days to be
> Bound each to each by natural piety.

I'm with Wordsworth on this. And I suspect you really are too. Wordsworth doesn't stop to say exactly why the rainbow makes him feel like this, but I reckon we all know what it means for the heart to leap up. We're excited, exhilarated, thrilled, marvelling, suddenly lifted into a momentary mood quite different to our everyday one. And it's all good for the body and the spirit. A natural individual high, quite different to any substance-induced one or any crowd hysteria. Lots of landscapes, not just rainbows, can do this for us. And the thrill we might get out of reading a particular sentence or hearing certain notes of music or suddenly understanding something about a painting or having a sudden insight into the way the natural world works, are other moments when the heart leaps up. They're all mysterious because we can't quite put our finger on why we react the way we do.

In addition, the rainbow has built up a whole world of associations and stories about itself. The book of Genesis has the rainbow as a sign of the agreement between God and humanity, an arch of beauty linking heaven and earth. Or in *The Wizard of Oz* Dorothy sings 'Somewhere Over the Rainbow' in her longing for a place free from troubles, knowing that the marvellous rainbow signals it's there all right, but lamenting her own inability to reach it.

Rainbows are also a feature of the natural world like thunder or lightning or things falling or bridges staying up or trees in autumn colours, or, or …you name it. And we trust that natural phenomena like these can be explained scientifically. And it should also be exciting for us to understand these scientific explanations. They don't 'explain away' the mystery, the beauty, the automatically uplifting potential of such things. Maybe some people could look at a rainbow and grouch, 'That bloody sun on the raindrops again!' But I don't think there'd be many of them.

For the rest of us, I reckon the more we know about the rainbow, the more our hearts will leap up. The rainbow doesn't lose its mystery because we know what causes it. The suddenness of its appearance, that band of colours, the fabled pot of gold at the end of it, the marvel of its actual cause, will all fuel our delight.

Always. To go back to Wordsworth. I don't know a cleverer

idea in all poetry than his ending. And it's a double-header at that. First there's his great paradox *[a paradox is an apparent contradiction – thus when two positions seem irreconcilable they are referred to as a paradox]* of the Child being Father to the Man. Then he trumps that by saying he wants to keep on showing that same trust and obedience to the child that he was, the father of the man he now is. And don't be put off by that word 'piety'. It's an old Latin meaning - not saying lots of prayers, etc., but the filial *[meaning 'of the son'; referring to the respect that a son should have for the father]* respect that the Romans said children owed to their parents. Keep swooning over the rainbows.

7.

'Did human beings make up maths?'

THE PHILOSOPHER'S REPLY:

Professor Sir Roger Penrose received a Nobel prize for his work on mathematics. He is one of the greatest mathematical geniuses of the present age. He did a survey of the most important mathematicians in the world and 97 per cent believed that mathematics was discovered not made up by human beings. He described this belief as almost like an implicit religion – one that few mathematicians talk about yet one which almost all accept. This is highly significant. If maths is, indeed, discovered it means that not all truth is relative. The truths of mathematics are universal across the cosmos and, possibly, even in alternative universes, if there are any.

If the universe is claimed to be simply a cosmic accident that can be explained by chance and random processes, then the existence of mathematics as an absolute discipline underpinning the whole of reality (as it does) provides a real challenge. To those who believe in God or an intelligence behind the universe then it is a simple matter to say that this provides an explanation for the existence of mathematics as an absolute. If one starts by dismissing God, the issue becomes much more complex and difficult to explain. Where does the mathematics that seems to underpin the whole cosmos come from if the universe is, indeed, just a pure accident with no meaning or purpose?

It would be much simpler to say that mathematics is a system made up by human beings and is in no sense an absolute. However, this appears not to be the case.

PROFESSOR TOM MCLEISH FRS

Professor of Natural Philosophy in the Department of Physics, University of York

This is a very big and good question! As far as we can see, maths results are not made up but could not be otherwise - so they must be discovered. That is not the same as to say that maths proofs are not made by humans, they are full of human creativity, which means that you have to be very creative to be a mathematician. But that is like a creative explorer finding ways through a difficult and strange landscape with rivers and ravines and forests that get in the way. You would like a bird's-eye view or a map but you only know about where you are and where you have travelled so far, so the next step is creative. Or the canoe you fashion or the path you hack through. In the end you find the beautiful temples (like Fermat's last theorem which is discovered or found)! Or the Riemann hypothesis - most people think it is there somewhere, but no one has yet found a path to it.

But here's the thing – if mathematics is there to be discovered, then it is in some sense 'real', but it is certainly not material, not made of stuff. If there is at least one body of things - mathematical things - that exist but are not material. That is one of the reasons that your question is so important, as it shows that things can be real and discoverable without being material.

Professor Gwen Bellamy

School of Mathematics and Statistics, University of Glasgow

This question is at the heart of 'philosophy of mathematics'. As a working mathematician, i.e. as someone who does mathematics research day to day (tries to understand examples, discover and prove new theorems, etc.), I have no experience of this. Indeed, my only knowledge of the way philosophers try to answer this question comes from reading popular science books in school. My recollection is that there are two camps - the Platonists who believe that there exists an abstract mathematical world independent of human beings (that we describe in our mathematics), and the others who believe that human beings invent mathematics. If you Google 'platonic mathematics' you can read all about this. But the best way to think about it is that there are some people who believe that we discover mathematics and others who believe that we invent it.

The only thing I can add is my personal thoughts on this, based on the experience of doing mathematics. When I do mathematics, I feel very strongly that I am discovering mathematics - we discover a new theorem, or we discover that the answer to the problem is 42. We do not 'invent' the answer to a question. So, I always feel that I am exploring some mysterious landscape when I am doing mathematics. But if I try to think rationally about this, I think we clearly invent mathematics (so I am not a Platonist, though I pretend to be). We invent definitions and we explore the logical consequences. You may think that this only applies to abstract mathematics. After all no one can invent counting or 1, 2, 3. But even for counting, the more precise you try to make this - e.g. how does one prove that $1 + 2 = 3$? - then the more choice there is and the more we see that we invent certain things.

Formally, this is the problem of constructing the foundations of mathematics. Nowadays there are many foundations of mathematics. but as a working mathematician I don't care, because they all lead to the 'obvious' things we care about like $1 + 2 = 3$.

8.

'Greta Thunberg seems to be wonderful and to want to protect our planet but no adults take much notice of her. Why won't they listen?'

THE PHILOSOPHER'S REPLY:

Greta Thunberg is indeed wonderful! And you are right that few adults take any notice and even fewer will do anything about it.

It is interesting that Pope Francis has a very similar message to Greta Thunberg – I have no idea whether she has any religious faith and the Pope clearly has, but their messages are remarkably similar. Both realise the urgency of the situation, both are convinced that too little is being done. The Pope calls for people to renounce the search for 'more' all the time and to be willing to live simpler lives. He wrote an extraordinary encyclical (a letter to the members of the Roman Catholic Church of which he was, of course, the leader) called *Laudato Si'* in May 2015. Although the document is about the environment the Pope puts it in a broader setting – the challenge to the environment arises because of a 'throwaway culture', greed and selfishness and it is this that has to change. Pope Francis describes a relentless exploitation and destruction of the environment, for which he blamed people not caring, the reckless pursuit of profits, excessive faith in technology and political short-sightedness.

'Laudato si' accepts the agreed scientific position that changes in the climate are largely man-made: '*We know that technology based on the use of highly polluting fossil fuels – especially coal, but also oil and, to a lesser degree, gas – needs to be progressively replaced without delay.*' The Pope focusses on poverty and the environment together saying that the world must '*hear both the cry of the earth and the cry of the poor*'.

The encyclical ranges widely dealing with climate change, water, genetics, the elimination of animals and plants, the effects on the sea and the arctic, the damage to crop production and the devastating effects on millions of the poor round the world. It also deals with the failure to take '*cross-generational responsibility*' – in other words the failure of older people to safeguard the environment for the young. So, the Pope and Greta Thunberg are both strongly aware of the need to preserve the environment for the benefit of children – yet adults ignore their messages. Why?

The answer, sadly, has to do with the fact the political systems around the world tend to focus on short term aims. Politicians are too often concerned with themselves and with power so they will do anything to get elected. Without being in power, of course, little can be achieved. Policies, therefore, that have a negative impact on the prosperity of voters will not go down well. People have been told that their living standards can go on increasing and that relentless growth is possible. They think that more cars, more new electronic products, greater heating of homes and the like are a human right and that anyone who denies this right is to be rejected. The answer to your question comes down to selfishness.

People will listen to environmental concerns provided

any proposed changes do not really impact on them or their expectations. Sadly, the world does not work like that. Global warming will initially affect poorer countries but will soon affect even the most affluent. It is only when people can clearly see the catastrophic effect that global warming has on farming, on water supplies and the ability to live on planet earth that really significant action will be taken. Sadly, by then it may be too late.

BISHOP JOHN KEENAN
Bishop of Paisley, Scotland

In one way you could see Greta Thunberg as a modern day prophet a little like Jeremiah in the Bible. When he was a young man God appointed Jeremiah with a message for the people of his times. Unless they radically changed their lifestyles their nation was facing devastation. The people did not heed his words but attacked him with threats and insults until his prophecy was proved true. By then it was too late.

In a world where people choose to ignore the truth, prophets are called to bring it to their attention, and when people dilly-dally, prophets confront then with stark life or death choices. Because they do not have cast-iron proof of what they say it is understandable that people may have legitimate doubts about them, especially when other false prophets have come and gone with stories that were not true, but which made them popular, and advanced their own agendas. So, prophets have to put up with a lot of suffering for what they say but it only seems to make them stronger.

In our times, as a teenager Greta Thunberg intuitively grasped the reality and scale of the climate emergency and how urgently and decisively the world had to act. She has faced a similar response, but she knows the message she has and the world she cares about are too important to allow herself to be silenced.

The world has reacted in different ways, some good and some bad. Some have asked for more evidence and that is fair enough. They want to know the facts on which she is basing her claims. Others have asked how clear and decisive the science is and if other opinions are reasonably possible. Still others have become more convinced of her warning as they have seen the body of evidence grow. Others are alert to any false prophets or opportunists who might attach other political ideologies to her simple message with no scientific basis to their claims.

Sadly, of course, there are others who are very happy with the lifestyles they live, selfishly producing and consuming goods made from fossil fuels for their own excessive benefit without a conscience about its harmful effect on others in the world or in generations to come. They just want to live for themselves and for the moment and not to think about others. They make

GOD APPOINTED JEREMIAH WITH A
MESSAGE FOR THE PEOPLE OF HIS TIMES.

decisions based on what they want for themselves here and now and not on what is real and good for everyone. Because they put no control on their appetites they cannot begin to think about, much less accept, any argument or evidence that calls on them to change their lives. Instead, they prefer to undermine or silence the message or, worse still, attack the messenger so that they can carry on as they are.

The story of the prophets is usually one of people not listened to at the time but who sacrifice themselves for a better future for others to come. The good news is that usually they win in the end and are honoured by those who benefitted from their words and suffering long after they are gone.

9.

'The world seems a terribly cruel place. Baby birds keep being killed by other creatures and human beings suffer from terrible diseases like COVID. Why? What is the point of all the suffering and pain?'

THE PHILOSOPHER'S REPLY:

There are two approaches to this question. If one is an atheist, then life evolves solely through natural selection and the survival of the fittest – this leads to every species seeking to survive and the strongest, fittest and sometimes most intelligent individuals seeking to pass on their genes through successful mating whilst competing with others who are doing the same. Nature is 'red in tooth and claw' with every species seeking survival in a highly competitive environment. This leads to suffering as one species eats and preys on another.

If one is religious, then the above still applies as, clearly, animals do strive for evolutionary success and the world is, indeed, a grim place. The difficulty that believers have is how to account for this. Christians, Jews and Muslims claim that God is wholly good and all powerful (omnipotent), and yet evil exists. These seem to be contradictory. How can evil and suffering which is so obvious in the world be reconciled with an all-powerful and good God – still less a God that is meant to be loving as well?

Assuming the universe was created by the sort of God that religious people believe in, would it have been possible to eliminate all suffering and pain? The answer must obviously be 'yes'. The question is that if such a world was created, what would the price be? The one thing that is clear is that genuine human freedom would be impossible. If human beings have at least a measure of freedom they must be able to be virtuous, kind and compassionate – but they must also be capable of the most hideous atrocities. If people are to be capable of genuine love, they must also be capable of inflicting hurt and pain, otherwise they would be like programmed robots. A robot can certainly be programmed to be kind, but this would be a result of programming – it would not be genuine. A robot could be programmed to care for very young children or old people who cannot look after themselves. It would never lose its temper, would always speak with a patient voice, would play games, or attend to the needs of the person it is looking after while making sure they are safe and cared for. All these actions would be a result of programming not a matter of freedom. In short if human beings are to be capable of great love and self-sacrifice they must also be capable of great cruelty and breaches of trust.

There are two broader questions you could ask. First, is it worth the pain and suffering in the world in order to have freedom? If the alternative were to live in a world where there is great beauty, love, compassion and where everyone is programmed to always be 'nice' and never 'nasty', would this be preferable to a world with the same beauty, love and compassion but also with the possibility of ugliness, hatred, cruelty and malevolence – in other words a world where genuine freedom is possible. Which would you prefer?

Secondly, if there is a life after death and this life is a preparation for a such a life then this changes the equation. In J. K. Rowling's *Harry Potter* books, Lord Voldemort is convinced death is the end and will do anything to avoid this including making copies of himself (Horcruxes) to enable him to survive death even though this means killing people to do it. He claims there is 'no good or evil, only power and those too weak to use it'. By contrast his opponents see death as the next great adventure and greet it without fear and stand for all that is good and worthwhile in the world. If this world is a preparation for the next, then the whole question of suffering changes and raises the issue of whether any life after death is worth the price of the appalling suffering that undoubtedly takes place in this world. There is no easy answer to this.

Dr Sue Price
Margaret Beaufort Institute, Cambridge

Ah, this is such an important question for it is one which has kept scholars and theologians busy for many years! The way I understand suffering and pain is to begin by saying first of all that I am not sure that there is a point to suffering, and I am absolutely convinced that God does not will suffering on anyone or anything. However, there is suffering, and really terrible things do happen to people, animals and nature. It is a good and important question to ask why these things happen. My explanation goes like this:

First and foremost, God desires us to be truly happy and to be perfectly made in His Image. However, we are human and not God, and because we are human, we can only be truly happy and perfectly made in His image when we are with God in heaven. On earth, we have a muddled understanding of what it means to be perfect (think of advertising) and what we think it means to be happy – again, think how advertising tempts us all into thinking we can only be really happy if we have this particular car, wear these particular clothes, drink this particular drink, etc.

God's perfection and happiness is very different – it is about our relationship with God, ourselves, each other, and nature, which becomes so full of love that there is no room for anything else. However, our very human nature means that we find that difficult to do here on earth. We keep trying, but because we and the whole of creation are not yet made in God's perfect image, where there is nothing else but love, suffering happens. The important thing is to keep trying to love as perfectly as we can. That kind of loving is important for it helps us to get through the difficult suffering times, holding fast onto God. And God understands the pain and cost of suffering, He loved us so much that He sent His own Son to us, who suffered because he became fully human as well as being fully divine. The answer to your question then is to say keep on loving everyone and everything as fully as you can, that loving is the way God can be with us in our imperfect, suffering world.

10.

'Why is it wrong to eat horses and not sheep or cows?'

WHY IS IT WRONG TO EAT HORSES AND NOT SHEEP OR COWS?

WHO SAID IT WAS NOT WRONG?

THE PHILOSOPHErS' rEPLY:

There is no reason for being willing to eat cows, calves and young lambs and not horses. The French eat horses; Australians eat kangaroos; South Koreans eat dogs; in Japan whale meat is a delicacy; in China many different animals are eaten or used as medicines (for instance the horns from rhinos); many rich people eat caviar which comes from the eggs of sturgeon (a type of fish). These are purely cultural prejudices passed on through the generations. Most (not all) religions have sanctioned the killing of some animals (Hindus regard cows as sacred, Muslims and Jews will not eat pork).

The Restaurant at the End of the Universe is the second book in *The Hitchhiker's Guide to the Galaxy* comedy science fiction series of six books by Douglas Adams. The restaurant has 'sentient food' including The Ameglian Major Cow (also referred to as the Dish of the Day) which was one of a number of artificially created, sentient (meaning they could think and be conscious) creatures, which were bred to want to be eaten, and who points out to the diners the merits of different parts of its anatomy so they could choose which to eat. At least this cow consents to be eaten (although given that it was bred for this purpose it probably had little choice but to choose to become food since this would have been part of its breeding!).

I have worked (as an auditor) in an abattoir and am well aware of the fear and distress as cows wait to be killed so the distress of animals being killed for food is all too clear to me.

Many films in the last twenty years have featured robots or A.I. that are self-conscious and clearly as much aware as humans are of their situation (think '*I, Robot*', etc.). There is now a lively debate among philosophers as to whether human rights should also be extended to Artificial Intelligence or, indeed, to alien life forms who may or may not be far more intelligent than we are. Such a debate is important, but the issue of extending human rights to animals is often ignored.

So, to briefly answer your question, there is no basis for eating cows and young lambs rather than horses but maybe if we are concerned with consciousness and the ability to feel pain we should not be eating either. This would solve many of the problems of global warming due to the decreased methane emitted, particularly by cows, but, politically, this will be almost impossible to achieve except by individual action.

REVD DR RAINER HAGENCORD

Director of the Institute for Theological Zoology, Munster, Germany

Every day, around 180 million land animals are killed worldwide for food purposes. Every animal that ends up in the slaughterhouse suffers enormously there after being denied a decent life. Modern animal husbandry violates basic Christian values. It wipes out entire populations and species of wildlife, locks up a large number of animals in factory farms in miserable conditions, damages the environment through the emission of methane from cows, wastes scarce resources and harms people's health. How is it that we are often blind to this suffering? Why does the Church not take a stronger stand in this matter? I would like to ask a counter-question to the one you raised: who says that it is not wrong to eat young lambs? Whenever the first lambs are seen in the pasture in spring, I stay with them and their mothers for a long time and am very deeply moved, usually the tears come to me for two reasons: They are pure innocence, manage to get on their feet very quickly and entrust themselves completely to their mother. A picture of the greatest joie de vivre and trust - I would like to have more of that myself! And then I think of the path they have to take: to the slaughterhouse! Then tears of anger come to me!

We live in a culture where compassion for animals is dismissed as sentimental; lambs, chickens, pigs and calves are degraded to 'farm animals'. This brutally cuts the ribbon that connects especially children with the other animal children. Brutality and violence against animals are becoming the norm.

There are other cultures on this earth in which violence is fundamentally renounced; no line is drawn between permitted violence against animals and illegal violence against humans. We can learn a lot from them!

Dr Peter Jones
Quaker and retired teacher of comparative religion

Speaking as a vegetarian since I was a teenager, I think it's wrong to eat all animals, using the Buddhist definition of 'sentient being' *[a being that has intelligence and is self-aware]* as this covers seafood and insects too. I do however admit that this is not always possible for everyone on this planet, but I do rule out any rearing of animals for eating that involves cruelty, specifically all factory farming. However, your question was more specific and here we are dealing with culture as well as religious beliefs. All over the world, meat eaters seem to observe certain taboos for a variety of reasons. You refer to cows, presumably because you are thinking about orthodox Hindus who believe the cow is a sacred animal. When I was in India and asked about this, my Hindu friends explained that the cow is important as a source of milk, that its dung is used as fertiliser or when dry, to use as a ground or floor covering, and that the animal as a bullock is used to pull conveyances. Horses are a bit different. In some countries, it is apparently okay to eat horsemeat, while in others no one would dream of eating it. I grew up in England, where horse meat was either used for pet food or exported to countries in Europe where they did eat it, like Belgium. This puzzled me as a lot of people didn't seem to mind betting on horse racing, even when horses were often fatally injured or just got put down when their racing days were over, but then they didn't want to eat them.

I travelled a lot when I got older and found that there were many other cultural and religious taboos on eating certain animals. Jews and Muslims didn't eat pork because apparently God told them not to, while friends in Ecuador told me that guinea pigs were a delicacy there while we always used to joke about the French eating frogs and snails. Later when I came to travel in Asia, I heard about people in Korea and Viet Nam eating dog meat as a delicacy while the Japanese ate whales and objected when other countries told them not to!

So there it is, not just cows or horses, but all sorts of other living creatures too, so I suppose you have to decide for yourself what you can or can't eat when you travel. I still reckon that if you can live without causing pain or suffering to living creatures, then that is the best path to follow, as we have all the alternative food sources available, and at Christmas I certainly feel sad that so many turkeys and chickens and geese have to die, let alone pigs for ham.

catrina younG
Deputy Head, Dixie Grammar School, UK

The answer to this question is, I would say, surprisingly simple - it isn't! In terms of evolutionary development there can be little, if any distinction, between the two creatures. This contrasts with eating snails, for example, that can be argued to have a less developed nervous system and therefore be unable to suffer to the same extent as cows and or horses. Furthermore, from a religious perspective there are no distinctions between the species unlike the Judaeo-Christian tradition that subscribes a fundamental sanctity to human life *['sanctity of life' refers to*

THE UNIVERSE AND THE NATURAL WORLD

*the belief that human life, as distinct from animals life, is 'holy'
and that it is never right to kill an innocent human being]* that
distinguishes us from other animals or the Hindu tradition
where the cow enjoys such reverence.

The more interesting question therefore is surely why
people, at least in Britain, *think* it's wrong to eat horses but not
cows? The reflection on scripture above shows the contextual
or relative nature of such value judgements; a horse burger
would be far more acceptable than its beef equivalent in many
societies. In the UK most horses enjoy the status of pets and
as such are usually ascribed names, cows rarely enjoy such
privilege and interestingly when they do are usually dairy
animals. This demonstrates the power that language has in
reflecting value - consider the difference between 'unborn baby'
and 'products of conception' both terms used, albeit in different
contexts, to describe a foetus in the early stages of pregnancy.
Culture clearly plays an important role in informing what is
acceptable and what is not - few Britons would choose to eat
sheep's eyes, yet in parts of the Middle East they are considered
a delicacy and served as a great honour to the most important
guest. In France, just 21 miles away from the UK, horses are
widely eaten and enjoyed.

If relativism *[the belief that all ideas of morality, of what is
right and wrong, depend on culture and there are no absolute]*
and cultural norms are to dominate this debate does that
mean there are no grounds for moral consideration? I
wonder whether instead of considering which animals can
be eaten a more pertinent moral question should be in what
circumstances may any animal be eaten? The conditions in
which the animal lives and is slaughtered is, for me, of greater
moral significance than whether it is a horse, cow or indeed a
guinea pig. Many would take the moral debate further still and
ask on what grounds we consider it ever appropriate to eat any

animal. Are there grounds to hold that humans are in some way superior and can therefore use animals to their own ends? The Bible suggests this is the case with Genesis describing God as giving Adam dominion over all other creatures but you do not need to engage in much biblical scholarship to acknowledge the difficulty with a literal understanding of the text - it is clear to many that within Genesis we have written the views of a society that had already established superiority over animals and would therefore inevitably see animals as suitable food for humans. Even if we accept human superiority, how are we to distinguish between different humans? The case for vegetarianism has been strengthened in recent years by our increased awareness of the environmental impact of meat production. On what grounds can we justify our enjoyment of meat today knowing that it has direct impact on the suffering of future generations?

11.

'Why do we find snow, clouds, small animals and flowers in spring beautiful?'

THE PHILOSOPHER'S REPLY:

There is no doubt that all of us regard some things as beautiful. The crucial philosophical question is whether beauty is something constructed by human beings dependent on our culture and upbringing or whether beauty is an absolute (in other words something that does not depend on culture or upbringing) that we learn to recognise – although, perhaps, in different forms in different societies. I dealt with this issue in Question 6. The great Greek philosopher, Plato, considered Beauty to be an absolute – just like Justice and Truth. The Christian saint, St Anselm, was later to argue for this position when he maintained that in every society in the world it is possible to put in order examples of justice and injustice and there would be almost universal agreement about these across all societies. In the case of Beauty it is more complex as ideas of beauty do vary across society – but this still leaves open the question whether these different understandings of beauty nevertheless point to an absolute value underpinning the universe.

As I have said in answer to another question, sometimes, very rarely, a mathematician will describe a proof as 'beautiful'.

This means that the proof is elegant and completely convincing. Once understood, it may even be simple – it is simply 'right'. To talk of a proof being beautiful is one of the highest marks of regard that a mathematician can make and, just as mathematics is widely regarded as something we discover rather than create (see Question 6), so beauty may be the same.

Personally, I am in awe of the incredible beauty found in the natural world – from the beauty of a bird's feathers and flight, the beauty of a snowflake, the beauty of a natural scene and many more instances. Sometimes when young children enter a great Cathedral for the first time they will look up and many will say 'WOW'. They are awe struck by the magnificence and grandeur of the building that may have been erected 800 or more years ago. They have not been taught to react like this – it is instinctive. The same happens when someone goes out at night on a clear evening in an isolated place where there is little light pollution and looks up at the stars. Awe, beauty, and wonder are connected. My answer to your question is that we find those things which you list beautiful because they are beautiful. We recognise something – it speaks to us, or at least it can do, at a deep level. I accept that this is not a proof, and some people may never feel awe and wonder at the beauty of the world. I can feel sorry for them, but this is not a proof that they are wrong and I am right – although I confess that I think they are mistaken and missing this experience or, perhaps, having it educated out of them is an impoverishment.

PROFESSOR CHRISTOPHER INSOLE

University of Durham and Australian Catholic University

Imagine that someone asks you to tell them what it is about your life that you find important and significant. You might talk about the people you love, or the places that are special to you, or your hopes and plans for the future. These things *really matter* to you. More than that: they *really matter,* because you matter. But now look at yourself in a different way: as a tiny speck in a vast universe, which has existed for billions of years without human life, and which will probably continue to do so in the future. From this perspective, our lives can suddenly look insignificant and unimportant. The feeling can be a bit dizzying. The two ways of thinking of ourselves are difficult to hold together.

The eighteenth-century philosopher Kant had some thoughts about this, and about how we might feel more 'at home' in the vast universe that we occupy. Kant asks us to think about what must happen before you can have even a very simple experience, such as seeing something red, or seeing a tree. He points out that all sorts of things must be in place: the world has to be rule-governed, so that objects continue to exist in a reliable way, so that we can expect the tree that was there this morning, to be there in the evening. We need to have certain regularities in nature, so we know that the pavement will not sink beneath our feet into an abyss. Also, we need to have minds that are capable of experiencing this world in a way that we can grasp and make use of.

For all of this to happen seems, Kant thinks, incredibly unlikely. But – it has happened! Even in a simple act of perception, something remarkable has occurred, which should give us a sort of pleasure and delight. Then, when we experience something which has a lavish amount of order, beauty, and harmony then we feel even more at home in the universe. Kant particularly praises flowers from the list above – he likes the mathematical structure of the petals - but it works for snow and clouds also. These things have a sort of excess of harmony, structure, and integration. That we find things beautiful, Kant thinks, gives us a deep hope that the universe is somehow 'for us', a proper home for us. Kant also notices that when we appreciate something as beautiful, we don't necessarily want to do anything to it, or with it: we just enjoy it. Consider the contrast with a tasty-looking cake, where we want to eat it. That we find things beautiful is a sign, Kant says, that we are capable of a sort of selflessness *[in other words ignoring self-interest and putting the interests of other people in first place]*, which we also need when it comes to morality. So, beautiful things make us feel at home in the universe and reveal to us our moral nature.

12.

‘There are billions of galaxies and billions of stars in each galaxy. If God created the world for human beings could it have been done rather more simply?’

THE PHILOSOPHER'S REPLY:

The universe has existed for over 13 billion years. There are billions of stars in our galaxy and innumerable galaxies. The development of the universe is certainly a long, drawn-out process. Science and human understanding of how the universe works is only possible because scientific experiments can work out, with great difficulty and over time, something of the nature of the universe and how it works. If this is the case, the universe has to obey clear laws (even though it may take human beings a very long time to even begin to understand how the universe operates).

We now know that the initial singularity had to be incredibly precise (see Question 1) and it is only because of this precision that the initial gases could form which would eventually coalesce and form stars and it is in the nuclear fires of stars that carbon is formed. It is out of the carbon that human beings and much of the natural world is formed. These processes cannot be hurried.

One of the most extraordinary things is that the human race which has evolved over millennia on a small planet circling an average size star, one of billions in an average size galaxy (of which there are, again, billions) can actually begin to understand the incredible complexity of how the universe works. The very fact that this is possible verges on the miraculous and it is only because the universe appears to obey very clear rules and laws. It did not need to be like this. Random events could have occurred which would have made prediction and science impossible. Instead by careful scientific work and testing over generations our species has been able to understand something of the unbelievable complexity of the universe. The new Webb Space Telescope which cost about 10 billion dollars will enable us to see further back in time to the very beginnings of the universe. All these discoveries and advances are possible only because the universe obeys rules.

The short answer, therefore, is that God (if God exists) is not a magician with a magic wand able to create random events which could not be explained. Instead, the universe shows all the marks of intelligence and purpose. If God exists, God is in no hurry and is not dominated by time in the way the short lives of human beings are. Instead the universe is full of beauty and wonder and provides the opportunity for us, as an apparently small and insignificant species, to discover at least the beginnings of how the universe comes to be. There is still a long way to go, but the fact the science is possible is, in fact, really quite extraordinary.

DR AILEEN A. O'DONOGHUE

Henry Priest Professor of Physics, St Lawrence University, New York, USA

The Christian religion has passed on the idea that 'God created the world for human beings', but to answer the question you pose, we need to consider the universe, not just the world that most of us equate with the Earth.

As you say, there are billions and billions of stars that we're now fairly certain all have planets. Human beings evolved on this planet in the Milky Way galaxy, but we have no information that we are the only species that evolved to the point of a civilization that has developed and handed on faith in God to us. Given the vast number of other galaxies, stars, and planets, there is no compelling reason to think that there aren't other civilizations in the universe (however difficult or even impossible for us to learn of and contact each other) that also develop faiths claiming that God created the world for them. Perhaps they also ask why God created all the other galaxies, such as our own Milky Way.

One of the greatest attributes of the universe, the Earth, and God, is exuberant abundance. The universe abounds with galaxies, each galaxy abounds with stars, most of which abound with planets, some likely very much like the Earth. The Earth abounds with life in an uncountable abundance of forms from microbes living inhabiting every crevice from within rocks in the dry valleys of Antarctica, to the Black Smokers so deep in the ocean that no sunlight penetrates to them. All these give evidence that God delights in exuberant abundance and the wonderful diversity that emerges from the self-creating systems it spawns.

Why create all the stars and galaxies? For the pure delight of watching what develops in each one. In our spiritual journey, I believe God calls us to delight in the abundance, too, and rejoice in being part of such a vast and amazing universe.

HOW DO I MAKE SENSE OF WHAT IT MEANS TO BE HUMAN?

13.

'What is a human being?
Is there a separate soul and
what evidence is there for this?
Surely the brain can explain
everything about a human
being without the need
for a soul.'

THE PHILOSOPHER'S REPLY:

Many would say that human beings are simply advanced animals. We share by far the greater percentage of our DNA with other mammals. We mate and breed in the same way; give birth in much the same way; females feed their young in the same way; we care for our young as many mammals do and seek to protect them when they are vulnerable. The evidence in favour of evolution through natural selection is exceptionally strong. If this is the case, then surely we can explain everything about a human being in material terms? The arguments in favour of this position are strong – but they are not conclusive and there are persuasive arguments in favour of the idea that human beings belong in a different category to animals. It is this belief that underpins the idea of the sanctity of human life.

WE SHARE BY FAR THE GREATER PERCENTAGE OF OUR DNA WITH ANIMALS.

Peter Singer is a prominent atheist philosopher who rejects religion entirely, rejects the idea of Sanctity of Life and argues instead for ethics based on the Quality of Life. What matters, he argues, in common with other utilitarians, is to maximise pleasure and happiness and to minimise pain and misery. He is therefore in favour of largely unrestricted abortion and euthanasia or assisted suicide if that is what an individual wants. Singer is a vegetarian and maintains that human beings cruelly oppress animals and cause them pain and distress. His argument is that we should stop being 'speciesist' – in other words treating human beings differently from animals simply because they belong to a different species. We would rightly condemn someone who was racist or sexist – being speciesist, Singer argues, belongs in the same category. Humans are not essentially different from animals.

Many people have put animals that they cared for out of their misery when they were suffering and in pain and did so because they cared for the animal – whether this be a dog, cat, horse, donkey, rabbit or guinea pig. If we do this, then Singer argues that we should do the same for human beings. If, therefore, a baby is born that is badly disabled, Singer would advocate killing it and having another baby whose 'quality of life would be better' than the one we killed. Most people would have a profound moral repugnance to this and Singer replies by saying this is an emotional not a rational reaction. His rejection of the Sanctity of Life goes right to the heart of the rejection of the ethics of all religions.

Perhaps, however, Singer is mistaken. We still cannot even begin to explain human consciousness. We can certainly measure brain waves and realise that certain areas of the brain are active at certain times and not at others, but we have no idea what consciousness is still less how to explain it. Human beings have developed art, music, poetry, architecture and have an innate sense of wonder at the beauty of the natural world which is shared by no animals. They also have an innate sense of a transcendent dimension to reality.

So, is there any evidence for a soul? If we mean by the word 'soul' a distinct physical part of the body (as René Descartes once held) then the answer is clearly 'no'. But if we mean by a soul the essential essence of a human being which is infinitely precious and important and which represents the core of who we are, then the evidence for this is strong. To seek to explain this essence, this core of our humanity, away by reducing consciousness to brain states is to trivialise the most important part of what makes us humans. Although Singer's arguments are powerful, the best argument against him is actually a theological one: that human beings are the pinnacle of God's creation and we are made in the image of God. But, of course, Singer as an atheist would reject such an argument.

BISHOP JOHN KEENAN

Catholic Bishop of Paisley, Scotland

The most important answer to this question is that we are a mystery. That does not mean we are unintelligible, but that there is a great wonder to us as yet unrevealed.

It is a question that religions, philosophers and scientists have tried to answer, uncovering more as time goes on. Still, none has reached the end of who we are, where we come from, where we are going and the meaning of our lives. In the end, the Psalmist thought the best answer was: *For the wonder of who I am I praise you!* (Ps 139:14)

What makes human beings such a puzzle is that, while there is something material to us, we also discover something within us that goes beyond the limits of matter.

With our bodies we share in the material world of rocks, plants and animals. Our bodies probably evolved into the complex organisms they are today and, with other living things we feel and move, grow through nourishment, decay and die.

And yet, while all other animals are content to live and die within the material environment that determines them, human beings are different. We find something inside us that takes us beyond the limits of our given environment. While other animals recognise their food, we give it a name. While cows in the fields are happy to remain chewing the cud, we plant seeds and expect harvests months away. We build mills to crush the grain, make recipes for bread and fire from flint to cook our meals. You have never seen a bull go off and explore but we have built spaceships and gone to the moon.

So, while other living creatures are contentedly controlled and directed by their environment, we have this remarkable capacity to transcend our material environment and create new ones in a never-ending adventure to understand our

Universe. It is this capacity that has even endangered our natural environment to the point of collapse.

Ancient philosophers recognised this puzzling capacity in humans and put it down to a soul, or life and organising principle that was other than material. Through this spiritual soul we were not stuck in the 'here and now' but could take ourselves to anywhere, anytime. Our minds were free and not determined by the limits of the environment. And, just as this freedom lets us think beyond material considerations, so it allows us to feel beyond our emotions and attain to genuine love in which others are not just things to satisfy our needs, but persons of infinite value.

That is why religions point out that we live in a spiritual environment as much as a material one that looks to some personal spiritual source to guide us, which they call GOD. Who makes our being and destiny even more mysterious and wonderful. As St John says: *we are already children of GOD but what we are in the future is still to be seen* (1 Jn 3:2).

14.

'What is the point of being alive?'

THE PHILOSOPHER'S REPLY:

Very few philosophers think there is no point in being alive. Albert Camus argued that life has no meaning beyond that which we create. It is impossible to arrive at any meaning for life but instead of getting depressed about this we should embrace meaninglessness. Human life is absurd and pointless. Camus, however, saw enjoyment in little things including sunshine, kissing, dancing and food and he loved football. A meaningless life can still be an enjoyable life.

The idea that life is meaningless, however, is very much a minority view and one which almost all major philosophers would reject. What is, perhaps, surprising is the amount of agreement there is between philosophers who support different views. Those in the Natural Law tradition of ethics (this holds that all human beings share a common human nature and actions are right or wrong in so far as they help us to fulfil or move away from the common human potential we all share) such as Aristotle and St Thomas Aquinas argue that we need to live according to the virtues and avoid those actions that diminish us and draw us away from our potential. Aquinas, as a Christian, believed that this potential was fully realised after death whilst Aristotle saw the potential to be fully human realised in this life. For

Immanuel Kant, human potential and meaning was to be found in living rationally and not allowing ourselves to be dominated by emotions or instinct. Kant saw this as a path to human fulfilment.

Utilitarianism is a secular ethical theory that sees the aim of life as to be happy and to avoid pain – but this does not mean a trivial sort of happiness that one might find after a good party on a Saturday night. Indeed, John Stuart Mill, one of the most influential Utilitarians, argued that those who seek their own happiness will not find it. For Mill, the aim of life should be to devote oneself to altruism – in other words the good and the happiness of others. If one does this one will, almost by accident, discover one is happy in terms of living a fulfilled life.

Those who put themselves in first place and seek trivial pleasures will find these disappoint and will end in despair.

SOREN KIERKEGAARD ARGUED THAT
MOST PEOPLE LIVE POINTLESS LIVES
OF QUIET AND SOMETIMES UNRECOGNISED
DESPAIR.

Indeed, Søren Kierkegaard argued that most people live pointless lives of quiet and sometimes unrecognised despair – but this does not need to be the case. All major religions recognise this, even if only implicitly. I rarely bring my personal experiences into any philosophic argument but after quite a long life I find that those who are most at peace and most happy are those who are committed to others rather than themselves. If we look at some of the greatest figures in recent history such as Nelson Mandela, Martin Luther King, Desmond Tutu and many, many more one will find people with a very high social conscience and a real commitment to the good of others – as well as being people who can look back on their lives and find them to have been incredibly worthwhile. The same applies to the very simple person who cares for others in their community and is always thoughtful and thinking of the needs of others.

Dr Anna Abram

Principal, Margaret Beaufort Institute, Cambridge

Only a human being can pose and try to answer this question. I live with an Orange Rex Rabbit called Beau (short for Beaufort). As far as one can understand other animals, Beau doesn't inquire into the purpose of his existence. He just lives. He finds the point of being alive in eating, playing, hiding under the sofa when he is scared, resting when he is tired and interacting with other creatures including human beings. It seems that Beau is born with an instinct to preserve his life. Human beings have the same instinct too, though sometimes they find their suffering so unbearable that they question the point of their existence. Asking this question means asking about the purpose and meaning of human life in general and

BEAU DOESN'T INQUIRE INTO THE
PURPOSE OF HIS EXISTENCE.
HE JUST LIVES.

individual life (the point of my own life). Human beings want to know why they live and for what purpose. Someone who believes in God, gods or any divine spirit is likely to see their existence as God-given. They tend to see life as continuous, stretching beyond death or life as we know it in this world and continuing into afterlife. For a Jewish or Christian believer, for example, the gift of life is an expression of God's love. It is something very precious.

Each person participates in the life of God and reflects God's own image. Each person's life is also unique. The appropriate response to the gift of life is gratitude. Those who don't believe in God or deity are likely to answer this question without referring to God or anything greater than what human capacities can capture. For many of them, life is seen as a gift too. It is not something we have chosen for ourselves or been given because of some merit. It is a mystery which we simply come to possess. To reject it would be a sign of ingratitude and a lost opportunity. To refuse it would go against our nature. So, whether we are a believer or not, we respond to the gift of life (like Beau the rabbit) by fulfilling our nature. Our goal as human beings is to fulfil our potential or to flourish and be at our best.

The Greek philosopher Aristotle introduced something called the 'Function Argument' to explain how to achieve this goal. He uses the analogy of a good harpist. For example, if Amy wants to be a good harpist, she needs to learn the skills how to play the harp. She also needs the instrument to practise. Interestingly, Aristotle does not suggest that Amy needs to question what the point of being a harpist is. He probably takes it for granted that being a harpist is a good thing. In the same way, Aristotle doesn't want us to worry too much about the question of what the point of being alive is. For him, the key question is how a human being should live or function. He proposes that human beings function well when they live according to the virtues (justice, practical wisdom, courage, etc.).

Aristotle agrees that other conditions need to be in place too. So, we need to eat, play, feel safe, keep healthy, have friends, etc. – as in the case of Beau the rabbit. These activities are part of our nature too. But, unlike Beau, we have more complex needs as well. Moreover, unlike in the case of Beau, we might not be fortunate enough to have the right conditions for leading a healthy and pleasant life. We or those around us might be sick or living in a place affected by war or natural disaster. Still, even in such places and circumstances, individuals can express courage, wisdom, kindness and care. Such basic activities as food, shopping, Facebook and WhatsApp interactions are not enough even if they bring some joy and fun. We want to know and learn things and ask deep questions such as the ones this book addresses. We want to receive love and care from our family and friends. We also want to show care for them and others including our animal companions. We are happy or fulfilled when we are good. Being alive gives us an opportunity to be good that is to be loving, caring, fair, courageous and so on. We only have one life. However long or short this life is, whether we are young or old, the ultimate point of it is to be good.

PROFESSOR TOM MCLEISH FRS

Professor of Natural Philosophy in the Department of Physics, University of York

Where do you think 'the point' of anything comes from? This is what we call 'purpose'. At the level of purely material 'stuff' there is no meaning to 'purpose' - not even passing on genes - that doesn't serve a 'purpose'; it just happens. If you want to ask that question AT ALL, then you need a framework, a world-view, a story that you live by, within which that question makes sense in the first place. And as soon as you do THAT, then there is potentially much more at stake than 'passing on genes'. Within the Christian framework that I live by, for example, the purpose of having children becomes part of a larger purpose for human beings, which is to look after the Earth, and each other, as little images of God who made it all in the first place.

15.

> **'**If we are just advanced
> animals what is the point
> of life, school, exams
> or anything?
> It all seems futile?**'**

THE PHILOSOPHER'S REPLY:

There are two key issues in this question revolving around the words 'if' and 'just'. If we accept that we are just advanced animals (as your question assumes) then we must dismiss the possibility of God or any transcendent meaning. If this is true, then there is no meaning or purpose to life other than that which human beings create. We are 'makers of meaning'. However, this does not mean that life is devoid of purpose but this purpose will probably be defined in terms of making life for humans and perhaps animals as pleasant and enjoyable and as pain free as possible. This gives rise to an ethical approach called 'utilitarianism' which is intended to maximise pleasure and minimise pain. The difficulty here is working out what 'pleasure' or 'happiness' mean. We can all think of times in our life that were happy, but this does not mean that we can define happiness. It is rather like trying to define a colour – we can think of examples of blue, red or green things, but this is not the same as defining them.

True happiness may well not be a series of happy

incidents but a fulfilled life – this was what the Greek philosopher Aristotle argued. A fulfilled life is one that fulfils human potential. However, we are back to the same problem as it is not easy to define 'fulfilment' or 'happiness'. Nevertheless, most of us can recognise a fulfilled life. These people do and did not seek their own happiness but rather seek and sought the very best for others and, in so doing, found fulfilment.

The second key work in your question is 'just'. Of course human beings are animals. We share almost all our DNA with other mammals, we reproduce in much the same way. Pigs, cows, dogs, cats, whales, wombats have sex in the same way we do. The embryo grows inside the mother until it becomes a foetus and finally a baby is born. After that the baby is suckled by the mother. The mother cares for the baby or babies until they can cope by themselves. The similarity to animals is unquestioned. The issue your question raises is whether humans are 'just' animals, and this is harder to answer.

Aristotle argued that human beings are different from animals because they can reason and are free. Religious believers might (or might not) also add that humans have souls. However, many animals are also rational (although to a lesser degree than most humans) and freedom in humans may be an illusion. We may think that we are free, but many people doubt this and maintain that freedom is just something that we think we have because we do not understand the complex factors that cause us to behave as we do. If we really understand enough about genetics and our upbringing, we will see that we have no freedom at all. This is an ongoing debate and is not easily resolved.

So perhaps we may be animals but also significantly more than animals: this, at least, is the religious claim and if this is correct then it is the 'more' that human beings are that becomes really interesting.

Even if we are 'just' advanced animals, there are still ways of living that contribute to the fulfilment of other human beings and perhaps also of animals. These are good, while ways of living that ignore the wishes or the good of others can be seen as wrong or damaging. They diminish us and lead us away from fulfilling our true human potential.

CARDINAL VINCENT NICHOLS
Archbishop of Westminster, England

In the Catechism of the Catholic Church our role in life is to love and serve God. In particular, (paragraph 293) we are told that the world was made for the glory of God. I remember that a few years ago, Pope Francis reminded us that the purpose of life is to live in God's 'fullness' and in the 'fullness' of creation. By doing this we can reflect on 'the joyful mystery' of 'the world' with 'gladness and praise.'

In this life we are on a pilgrimage, on a journey. Life is not the final destination in itself, it is just a part of the journey to the time of our *Dies Natalis*, a Latin expression meaning our birthday into eternal life. As Catholics, our hope is in the Resurrection. Instinctively we know that there is more to come. We have yet to achieve our true and deepest purpose.

In the language of faith, we recognise that the deepest structure of our being is to reach the fulfilment for which we have been created. Unless we embrace this, our journey leads to nowhere and is without any lasting meaning. God's grace infuses our natural hope – our stretching forth with restless hearts for the future good, difficult but possible to attain. Our home lies beyond us. Our hearts and our reason reach out to that home and the gift of God is what makes it truly attainable. In St Matthew's Gospel (10:39) we are told:

Whoever finds their life will lose it, and whoever loses their life for my sake will find it.

The word 'Gospel' means Good News. And the 'Good News' here is that by committing ourselves to following Christ, He will accompany us on our journey, offering support and consolation particularly in difficult times, when life seems full of problems and perhaps pressures at school, such as exams.

Life is far from futile! We have each been given gifts to use to glorify God, to serve Him, and to share His love with those around us. For God so loved the world that He gave his only Son, so that everyone who believes in him might have eternal life (John 3:16). So we are called to live our lives to the full in a spirit of Faith, Hope, and Love, (1 Corinthians 13:13) so that we may glorify God. This, then, is our prayer, our mission in life. Amen.

16.

'What does it mean to be happy? I'm not sure I know.'

WHAT DOES IT MEAN TO BE HAPPY?

THE PHILOSOPHER'S REPLY:

When Harry Potter sat in front of the mirror of Erised it was meant to show him what his heart desired most. For the majority of people that would probably be good health, happiness and success. As we have seen (Question 15) there is no agreement at all about what it means to be happy and there is even less agreement about the nature of success.

Most people might consider that it consists of a series of enjoyable events, maybe falling in love, marriage and having children, perhaps economic success measured in terms of the sort of house one owns, the car one drives or the amount of money one has to spend. Philosophers, however, have always recognised that these goals are illusions – they seem attractive but eventually disappoint. However wealthy, powerful or famous one becomes there are always people more so than you.

In Robert Bolt's play *A Man for All Seasons*, the then Lord Chancellor of England, Thomas More, was confronted by an ambitious young man who wanted to join his team; More looked at the young man and recognised that he was pursuing goals that would ultimately disappoint. He told the young man to be a teacher and said, if he was a good teacher, he would know it, his pupils would know it and God would know it. Even if one does not believe in God there is wisdom here. Living a life of service to others, putting self into second place, is the only real way to human fulfilment and happiness. It may not bring financial success or, indeed, fame but neither of these are ultimately important. When we come to die there are more important things – such as the sort of person one has become and what good one has done in the world. It is those who seek these latter goals that would find real happiness – not by seeking it but by looking for the happiness of others.

THE MOST REVD AND RT HON STEPHEN COTTRELL
Archbishop of York

The word happy has a fascinating etymology. Its root – hap - appears in such words as perhaps and happen; haply, happenstance and haphazard. It means chance, fortune, even accident. Something comes to pass, but not necessarily by design. It just happened! But could this be the root of happiness? Is the English language onto something? That we can't, in any ordinary sense, arrange for happiness; rather, as Robert Farrar Capon says in his excellent book on the subject, 'happiness must somehow befall us'.

Happiness, he argues, lies in our ability to accept what happens to us and to respond to it appropriately, recognising that we cannot control all that happens to us, but we can control how we choose to respond. Moreover, happy people, those who choose to respond in this way, seem to exhibit a joy that is both hugely infectious and deeply serious. Happiness is about the choices we make. Even when life is very hard. It's also why some of the happiest people I've ever met have been those living with the greatest hardships.

'Happy are the poor in spirit … Happy are those who mourn … Happy are the meek … Happy are those who hunger and thirst for what is right', says Jesus (Matthew 5:3-6).

This is the controversial translation of the New English Bible in the 1970s.

Oh the 'behappytudes' a grumpy member of my first congregation called them. But isn't this translation onto something? The Greek word *makarios* is usually rendered 'blessed' (an altogether far more serious and holy word); but 'happy' is just as good a translation. The word carries both meanings – to be blessed by God and to be filled with joy. The Beatitudes of Jesus make sense of our English word 'happy' by showing that joy is found by our choice to live our lives in particular ways. The beatitudes are vocations. They don't come naturally. But they do carry blessings. We see them lived out perfectly by Jesus himself. They are the way of life to which all of us are called. As the psalmist says: a path of life that leads to the fullness of joy (see Psalm 16:11).

So happiness is not easy or cheap. It is much simpler to turn away, than to turn the other cheek. But that won't bring happiness. As Paul writes, joy is complete when we have the same mind as Christ (Philippians 2:2 and 5).

To have the mind of Christ is to live and inhabit the world in a certain way; to choose to be merciful; to choose to be generous; to choose to be a peacemaker. When we make these choices and respond to life in this way, life won't be easy, but we will be happy. Happiness will befall us.

FATHER CHRIS GLEESON SJ
Staff Chaplain at Xavier College and former head of Riverview College, Sydney

The story is told of an old Cherokee warrior one evening telling his grandson about a battle that goes on inside all people. He said, 'My son, the battle is between two "wolves" inside us all. One is Evil. It is anger, envy, jealousy, sorrow, regret, greed, arrogance, self-pity, guilt, resentment, inferiority, lies, false pride, superiority, and ego. The other 'wolf' is Good. It is joy, peace, love, hope, serenity, humility, kindness, benevolence, empathy, generosity, truth, compassion and faith.'

His grandson thought about this story for a minute and then asked his grandfather: 'Which wolf wins?' The old Cherokee warrior simply replied: 'The one you feed.'

As a little boy I would often ride my bike down to the nearby shops in Sandringham to run messages for my Mother. The cake shop owner, the butcher, the greengrocer and the grocer all knew me and my brothers by name and delighted in carrying on conversations with us about all manner of things. They seemed to have plenty of time for us, even giving us broken biscuits or lollies when it so moved them. It was a far cry from today's check-out people who have been trained to roll out the impersonal, 'How's your day been?' Having a tetchy queue close at hand does not lend itself to an expansive response.

In contrast a few weeks ago, I met a young woman behind the counter at the local BP garage who really was interested in what sort of day I'd had. We shared a few sentences about my drab and dreary experiences, until her parting words echoed in my ears: 'I think it is very important to keep happy.'

'Keep happy.' Happiness is so much about attitude, about gratitude. That remarkable deaf and blind woman, Helen Keller, a role model for all of us in persistence against extraordinary odds, once wrote: 'Most of us take life for granted. Only the deaf appreciate hearing; only the blind realise the manifold blessings that lie on sight. It is the same old story of not being grateful for what we have until we lose it; of not being conscious of health until we are ill. But I, who am blind, can give one hint to those who see; use your eyes as if tomorrow you would be stricken. And the same method can be applied to the other senses; hear the music of voices, the song of the bird, the mighty strains of an orchestra, as if you would be stricken deaf tomorrow.'

Keeping happy has nothing to do with self-promotion, but everything to do with serving others. The blueprint for Christian behaviour in Matthew's Gospel account of the Beatitudes reminds us of this very forcefully: 'Happy those who hunger and thirst for what is right; happy the merciful; happy the pure in heart: happy the peacemakers.' This is like a litany of congratulations from God and is a far cry from the recipe for happiness proclaimed in the marketplace today: 'Happy are the glossy people, their bodies will be admired; Happy are those with spare cash they will be satisfied. Happy are the tough ones they shall achieve success'.

The old Irish proverb captures this very well: 'We live in the shelter of each other.' Keeping happy is about looking out for others. Caring for one another is what strong communities do. Indeed, John Paul II once pointed out very wisely that the quality of any community can be measured by the care it provides for its weakest members. 'None of us is as strong as all of us', was at one time the clever catch cry of fast food giant McDonald's. What a difference it would make to our world if we could all adopt the African philosophy of happiness expressed in the adage: 'I am because we are'! Keeping happy focuses on learning to value and respect others, even if we don't always get our own way or have our needs met. Keeping happy understands that life is about us, and not just about me.

In any strong community service organisation whose very lifeblood stems from caring for and serving others, keeping happy might almost be an habitual state of mind and heart for its members. Whether that be true or not, those people would know that their work for the needy and marginalised is an ongoing opportunity to meet Jesus face to face. 'I tell you solemnly, in so far as you did this to the least of these brothers of mine, you did it to me.' And one can't get much happier than that!

THE REVD DR MARK OAKLEY

Dean, Fellow and Tutor, St John's College, Cambridge

I have to be honest. 'Happiness' is a word I dislike. Is it because it just sounds too sugary, and contaminated by self-help gurus or little yellow faces sent annoyingly in texts, in a world too knowing, too sophisticated, too ironical, too post-everything to take it very seriously? No, not quite. For beyond any sniggering, there is a restlessness that still yearns for the experience of contentment it is trying to define, that state of emotional balance we are in when not unhappy. Other terms for happiness are equally off-putting: 'subjective well-being' is awful, so are 'positive emotionality' and 'hedonic tone' - and 'wellness' sounds like a coastal town in Norfolk.

My dislike of the word 'Happiness' is more probably due to the fact that, implying it is a permanent state you can reach if you try, the word sits there, rather smugly, saying 'Here I am, others have found me why can't you?', when really I think it is playing a rather different game with us. This word 'Happiness' is a flirt, winking at us to follow but then leaving us stranded on the chase. Dumped as we are, we wonder who else is enjoying the experience instead of us and what did they do that we didn't?

The United States Declaration of Independence talks of the pursuit of happiness. The pursuit of happiness though - for itself - might be the very cause of unhappiness. This, I think, is true if you treat happiness as an end in itself and not something that can be enjoyed periodically whilst pursuing other ends. What those ends should be is a matter for debate and conscience.

Is happiness, that equilibrium of head and heart that lifts us out of unhappiness to a general contentment and stability, the ultimate good, the supreme state that might be entered if I do this or buy that, if I go there or look like that? Or is it a life lived between extremities, and avoiding the contagious culture of 'wanting'?

We are living today within a dangerous circle of spending money we don't have on things we don't want in order to impress people we don't like. The ads appeal to our ids, we end up personalising objects and objectifying people (so, in the adverts you never know if the man is having an affair with the woman or the car) and, doubting our worth, we create a culture of entitlement, attention-seeking, litigation. In the

'I am seen, therefore I am' culture of fame, where high self-esteem accompanies low self-awareness, injustice and matters of the 'common good' struggle hard to get in the news. Before long, our lives will reflect the game shows that cram up our channels: a monotonous drone of competition. To go native to this culture where means very quickly become ends, and wants are confused for needs, will, I think I can guarantee, not ever make us happy. Indeed, an integral part of happiness, as Bertrand Russell said, is to be without some of things you want.

I often return to the wisdom of the old man who was interviewed at the Glastonbury Festival. He was asked about happiness, whether it was something we feel or something we do. 'I'll tell you the secret to happiness', he said. 'I found it written on a bottle of bleach.' The interviewer reached for his pen, mouth open, poised. The old man whispered: 'Stand upright in a cool place.'

17.

'Why are people so concerned with fashions and the labels on clothes?'

THE PHILOSOPHER'S REPLY:

The power of marketing, the media and advertising are very great. People watch television where there are many advertisements, they watch films where products are 'placed' to emphasise their attractiveness, they visit shopping centres where the focus is on persuading people to buy things they may not really need. The purpose of marketing is to create a want in people's mind which can only be satisfied by a purchase. For many shopping is a major hobby. A want is turned into a 'need' and the need must be satisfied. This is, in essence, the drive behind materialism, consumerism and, indeed, capitalism. People always want 'more' and the 'more' they want is decided for them by shrewd advertising and promotion which targets younger and younger audiences.

There is, however, an even more important element and that is peer group pressure. If a society can be created that finds purpose and meaning in owning and buying things, then anyone standing against this inexorable trend will find themselves marginalised. Often this is seen in schools where it can sometimes be seen to be important to be wearing the 'right' brand of trainer, the 'right' brand of coat, the 'right' handbag or sports kit. The same applies with clothes – people who shop at cheap stores may find themselves looked down on by the insiders who can afford the 'right' kit.

Fashion labels on clothes contribute to this and, in order to keep their business going, new colours, new designs and a new 'look' are essential and those who wear 'yesterdays' look are sometimes looked down on. Most people are not even aware of how their desires are influenced and the pressure on them to conform – but the pressure is very great and standing against it is exceptionally hard and, indeed, rare. The film *The Devil wears Prada* illustrates this well.

The answer to your question, therefore, is 'because they have been manipulated to seek things and appearances that are trivial and of passing worth' but, of course, very few people other than philosophers or those who are poor (who have little choice) will accept this. The story is told of a great philosopher, Diogenes, who lived in a barrel and had no possessions other than a stick, a breadbasket and his barrel. Alexander the Great is meant to have visited the city where Diogenes lived and was told of the fame of the philosopher, so he went to see him. Standing before Diogenes, who was sitting beside his barrel, Alexander is reputed to have said: 'I am Alexander. Ask of me whatever you will.' To which Diogenes is meant to have replied: 'Stand to one side. You're blocking the sun.' In other words, there was nothing that Diogenes wanted. Alexander, impressed, is reputed to have said to his followers: 'Say what you like, but if I were not Alexander, I should like to be Diogenes.' They are reputed to have died on the same day – the one had immense and almost total power, the other had nothing – one might wonder who was the happier or more fulfilled?

THE RT REVD RACHEL TREWEEK

Bishop of Gloucester

Everyone wants to feel valued and accepted, and the advertising of beauty products and celebrity fashion is dominated by a message that your value is rooted in what you look like, i.e. if you look a certain way and wear certain clothes then you will be valued, belong and be happy. As a Christian, I want to bust that myth and say that our value and happiness doesn't begin on the outside but begins on the inside, knowing that we are precious and loved. The amazing truth is that no two people in the world are the same and every one of us is unique. I believe that we are all created in the image of God, that we are loved and known by name, and that when we go on discovering who we are and telling one another what we value in one another, rather than simply commenting on people's appearances, then our concern with fashion and designer labels might diminish. Of course, we can still enjoy fashion but it will become an expression of who we are on the inside rather than it being what defines us.

18.

‘Given how many relationships
fail, isn't it better to avoid
trusting anyone as then you
won't be hurt?’

THE PHILOSOPHER'S REPLY:

You are right: Many relationships do fail. The divorce rate is very high (well over a third of marriages end in divorce) and the rate of divorce for second marriages is even higher. Many couples 'fall in love', move in together and perhaps have one or more child only to find that their love has died. Sometimes couples will stay together for the sake of the children and will separate once the children have left home. The number of teenage romances that end is even higher so you are absolutely right to be cynical. The fact that many relationships do fail, however, does not mean they all do and perhaps more succeed than fail.

The problem comes from two major factors. Firstly, most people do not understand what the word 'love' means and secondly people live much longer than in the past and they change with the passing of the years. Let's deal with these in turn.

For many people (and most popular songs) love is an emotion – indeed it is a very powerful emotion. From the early teenage years onwards most human beings (like other animals) are programmed to breed and to select a mate, which will enable them to do this. In some countries today girls can get married very early and in centuries past this would have been the case in the Western world as well. The desire to find a mate (and hence, generally, love as a prelude) is very strong indeed. This biological and perfectly natural impulse is, nevertheless, no guarantee that a relationship will last. Being passionately in love, wanting the other person, enjoying the excitement of a new relationship and setting up house together are very different from the tedium of nappies, then school runs, paying bills, putting out the rubbish, coping with a leaking roof or losing one's job. The handsome young man and the beautiful young woman will change with the passing of the years and their habits can become at best trying, more often annoying and in some cases infuriating.

THE HANDSOME YOUNG MAN AND THE BEAUTIFUL YOUNG WOMAN WILL CHANGE WITH THE PASSING OF THE YEARS.

To say to someone that you love them can easily, therefore, be an expression of a perfectly genuine emotional reaction and the overwhelming feelings that this reaction generates can act like a pair of rose-coloured glasses through which everything about the other person seems wonderful and, even those things that may appear less attractive, are seen as comparatively trivial. The rosy glow generated by the genuine initial emotions can nevertheless fade into the plain light of day and as the emotions die so does the initial love. It may, of course, be replaced by something else – ideally a genuine and deep friendship and mutual sharing which enriches both parties and is precious and wonderful. This can then give rise to a wonderful and profound long-term relationship that grows in intimacy and understanding with the passage of the years.

In many ways it would be better if it were the other way round and genuine and deep friendship, fostered and tested over years, then grew into a deep love and understanding. This is often the basis for the best marriages that will stand the test of time and all the trials and tribulations that any relationship will have to overcome if it is to endure.

The second problem is that if someone marries in their mid-twenties, they are likely to live for perhaps sixty more years and both they and their partner will change radically during these years. They will meet other people, change jobs a number of times and most certainly change appearance. This means that love that is based on appearance or anything outward is unlikely to last.

Trust is one of the most important ingredients of a successful relationship which is why the breakdown of relationships and the betrayals involved are so very, very painful. To be able to say of someone, 'I am willing to trust him/her with my soul, my inmost thoughts, my happiness, my whole future and the happiness of any future children in the total conviction that this trust will not be betrayed' might be a better test than to ask yourself, 'Do I love him/her?'. Even then, of course, your trust may turn out to be misplaced or you may betray their trust – but, although these are possibilities, they are not necessarily the case.

It is worth being aware that when relationships break down the fault is rarely on one side only – when a number of relationships fail the fault (if that is the right word which is debatable) may not be with the other person but at least partly with you!

Grace Akosua Williams
Social entrepreneur and lawyer, Tasmania

Trust is vital for love. Just like a butterfly would die if she stayed in her cocoon forever, hearts wilt without trust. Avoiding trust is avoiding love, loving others and being loved is what makes life good. Imagine an anxious butterfly. As she hides herself in a cocoon, she can hear all of life singing to her, calling her name in an invitation to join the wonder outside, but the butterfly stays because it is safe. She cannot bring herself to leave her cocoon knowing there is no way of returning to the comfort of safety. By choosing to stay in her cocoon, she never sees the beauty of life and cannot know anything beyond the bounds of her small cocoon. By refusing to trust herself and trust life her wings are trapped, and she will never fly. A butterfly who does not leave the cocoon, can never truly become a butterfly and a human being that cannot trust never experiences the full breadth and depth of their humanity Trust is a sacred necessity - it is a gift we give to ourselves and to those we love. Giving something so precious as the gift of trust means learning to first be a trustworthy person, and then choosing the right person who respects the delicate nature of your heart. Trust is necessary for love in all relationships. Trust is what allows us to be safe in this world with one another. This does not mean giving your precious gift of trust to everyone, but it does mean you shouldn't withhold trust because you fear being hurt.

Although relationships pose great risks to our hearts, trusting ourselves to be strong enough to re-emerge from painful experiences is a part of living a life in intimate relationships with others. Knowing that who you are is much greater than the hurt inflicted on you by others means that you won't limit your expression of love by choosing to stay in a self-made cocoon. Many relationships fail because they embody our imperfect humanity, but our imperfections should not prevent us from being in trusting relationships. As imperfect beings we are always learning, changing, and growing so expecting our relationships to always stay the same is asking life to stand still when it is always changing. We cannot contain other human beings, any attempt to do so would be like trying to capture the wind in an open bottle.

You may meet someone who will break your heart and you may also meet someone who will treat your heart with the respect it deserves. This is the imperfect paradox of life.

19.

'Does the idea of seeking
truth make sense any longer?
Everyone seems to have their
own truths and we are told that
we must respect everyone's
views no matter what they are?'

THE PHILOSOPHER'S REPLY:

In 2016, Oxford University Press nominated 'post-truth' as the word of the year. This was a legacy from President Trump. At his inauguration as President he claimed that the crowds were greater than those at the inauguration of his predecessor – President Obama. The New York Times published photographs clearly showing that Trump's crowds were much smaller. His spokesperson said that Trump was presenting 'alternative facts'. This became a feature of his Presidency. He continually spoke lies and these were presented as 'alternative facts'. This mirrors the dominant view in modern society of relativism and postmodernism. Relativism claims that the days of absolute Truth (notice the capital 'T') are over and everything is relative to culture. Postmodernism claims that there is no longer any single meaning of a painting, a novel, a piece of journalism – everything depends on culture, sexuality, gender, race and similar factors. Relativism and postmodernism now hold such sway that the idea of absolute Truth is derided and mocked in many quarters.

It is a bit like Hans Christian Andersen's story of the Emperor's new clothes. An Emperor was sold a suit of clothes which, he was told by the tailors who made them, were incredibly expensive as they could only be seen by those who were wise. Naturally the King and his courtiers all admired the clothes as they did not want to appear foolish – they all said how beautiful they were and how well the colours matched. One day, however, the King went out in a procession through the town and everyone, again, admired the clothes until a little boy shouted, 'He's got no clothes on'.

Absolute truths do exist. It is either true or false that I had a cup of coffee this morning. It is either true or false that the atom is the fundamental element in the universe (it is false!). It is either true or false that Caesar ate an apple on the morning he landed in England (notice there is no proof – but it is still either true or false). Some people in 2021 held that the vaccine against COVID-19 was an elaborate plot to implant tracking devices into people's bodies or to render men sterile. This was either true or false – and it matters which is the case. All the evidence points to the fact that the idea of a plot was false, but many still believed it to be true and refused the vaccine, and many of these people died.

Truth matters – indeed, perhaps, it matters more than anything else. It may be difficult to arrive at truth and there are different perspectives on many issues all of which need to be recognised and all of which may contain an element of truth but this does not undermine the claim that absolute Truth (note the capital 'T') exists.

Professor Frank Brennan SJ

Human rights lawyer and academic, University of Melbourne

If you had a choice of the good, the true and the beautiful or the bad, the false and the ugly, which would you choose? If it were that simple, you would always choose the former, wouldn't you? Anyone who deliberately chose the latter would be a fool, a mad person or an evil one. What appears beautiful to one person might appear ugly to another. Beauty is in the eye of the beholder, as we say. Is it the same for truth and goodness?

No matter what age we are, we are still able to judge if the deed of someone else is good or bad, or perhaps neutral. We look at the person's motivations, their intentions, and the consequences of their action. It is a good deed for the child with good eyesight to assist the elderly blind person to cross the street. It is a bad deed for the same child to lead the blind person to the pedestrian crossing in the face of oncoming traffic when the crossing light is red.

We cannot judge all deeds of others being undoubtedly good or bad. There will be many deeds of others we cannot judge because we do not have enough information to make an informed decision. But there is no doubt that some deeds are good and some deeds are bad.

No matter what age we are and no matter what our level of intelligence and education, there are some things which are true and other things which are false. At the same time, there are many things which we cannot judge to be true or false. Some people might think something to be true, while others think it is false. In the past, most people thought that the sun rotated around the earth. This is false. Now most people think that the earth rotates around the sun. This is true. It makes sense to pursue and affirm this sort of truth. Possessed of this sort of truth, we are able to make all sorts of scientific predictions which would not be possible without reliance on this truth.

When we move from making true or false statements about nature and the physical environment, it can be more difficult to determine what is true and what is false. Some people think it is best to live one way and others think it best to live a completely different way. We need to respect the dignity of all people and to respect their life choices. We still need to make life choices for ourselves. It's not that all life choices are the same or equally true or equally untrue. While a life choice might be true for someone else, it will only be true for me if I judge it to be really true. I can respect the various life choices of others while still seeking the truest life choice for me. I need to be tolerant of others while being a keen seeker of truth for myself and those I love.

20.

' If we are going to have
children should we not
genetically engineer them to
minimise disease, mental illness
and other problems? **'**

THE PHILOSOPHER'S REPLY:

The ability to minimise pain and disease has been the object of all medicine since the earliest times. Today this ability has been increased with technology like CrispR which enables genetic alterations to be made to the early stage embryo.

There are two types of genetic engineering. The first seeks to use genetic modifications to treat existing diseases and to rectify things that have gone wrong with a person's body. This is like other forms of medicine which seeks the best interests of the patient. The alternative however – and it would seem this is what your question is about – manipulates the genes of an early stage embryo either to rectify what are perceived as defects (for instance genes associated with breast cancer or Down's syndrome) or to enhance particular features of a future human being (examples might be making the future adult taller or having a different eye or hair colour or, perhaps, minimising a disposition to violence or increasing intelligence). This second type of genetic engineering has only just begun and is still in its infancy. It is called germ line genetic engineering and it carries with it problems that do not exist in the first type.

First, any genetic alteration of an early stage embryo will affect every cell including reproductive cells which means that any alteration will pass on into the genes of future children. This carries real dangers as the alteration is irreversible – it will be part of the gene pool of future humans and we simply do not know enough to be sure of the dangers. Imagine, for instance, that a male foetus is genetically altered in some way in China and a female foetus is altered in a different way in the United States. The two foetuses grow to become babies, then children and then adults. They meet and have children. Their respective genetic alterations will pass onto their children and we have no idea whether they might react together in an unanticipated way. This is not like, for instance, a medicine that is found to have adverse effects and can then be withdrawn. Genetic alterations to humans will be passed onto their offspring and we do not know enough about what the long term consequences may be. The risk, in my view, is simply not worth the possible benefits.

Secondly, this technology will only be available to the wealthy and this would mean creating a genetic apartheid in which the children of the rich have inbuilt advantages that others do not, and this is likely to create major social problems.

Thirdly, there is no clear agreement about what should be allowed and what should not. Most people would support any genetic alteration that could eliminate the disposition to some forms of cancer but there is far less agreement about what abilities should be enhanced. There is no agreement between cultures about what constitutes beauty or success or intelligence.

The downsides, therefore, of the second type of genetic engineering seem to outweigh the supposed benefit. Having said this, it is almost inevitable that it will become increasingly common as there will always be parents who want what they consider to be 'best' for their children (however this is defined) and there will always be countries and doctors who will be willing to carry out requested alterations. This does not, however, make it the right way to proceed.

SISTER GEMMA SIMMONDS CJ, PH.D.
Director of the Religious Life Institute, Cambridge

There have been many wonderful medical advances which religious believers see as a way of co-operating with God's Spirit at work in the world through the brilliance of scientific discovery. In earlier times people died of what we now know are avoidable diseases, and this is still the case in parts of the world without access to clean water or vaccination programmes.

Engineering the human genome in a way that minimises disease and disability is now possible. In 2008 the Vatican published a document, *Dignitas Personae*, on what it sees as the rights and wrongs of this 'genetic engineering'. It called science 'an invaluable service to the integral good of the life and dignity of every human being.' So far, so good. The Catholic church is certainly not the enemy of science, and the historical figure Gregor Mendel, credited with being the 'Father of Genetics', was a Catholic friar. Preventing diseases or disorders that would cause great harm and suffering, is seen as good. But for one human being to decide that another person's life isn't worth living because of a defect or disorder, and to end their life before it fully begins, is seen as unacceptable.

This is what lies at the heart of some religious beliefs that question so-called genetic engineering. Who gets to decide what a worthwhile life is, and on what grounds? Some countries now legally abort babies up to full term when they are found to have Down's syndrome, or birth defects like a cleft palate, which can be easily remedied at birth. We are coming dangerously close to denying the intrinsic value of people who have such 'defects'. People who have Down's among their family or friends have often testified to the huge enrichment such relationships offer, as they learn to value the beautiful human virtues and attributes that people with Down's so often display. We learn to see vulnerability not as something to be avoided at all costs, but to be embraced and understood. To deny someone the right to life because their life is seen as being potentially of lesser value than another's is highly questionable. We already have some cultures where male babies are more highly prized than female babies. This can lead to gender-selective abortions and sexist attitudes that set girls and women at a huge social disadvantage.

Gene therapy that is aimed at the correction of a disorder is acceptable in principle, provided it respects and promotes the personal wellbeing of the person it is treating, from conception onwards. The religious view sees human beings as more than mere biological entities which can be modified or improved by any means and for any purpose. It requires the unique nature of each individual human being to be respected and protected. No harm can be involved in the process of that human being's generation, or their fundamental design altered. Equally, the marginalization of people with perceived 'disorders', whether physical or mental, is seen as a major injustice, always to be avoided.

21.

‘One of our relatives said that
we are simply advanced animals
with no meaning or purpose in
our lives. He told us about Elon
Musk and his efforts to implant
chips in our brains and said
that this may be the next step in
evolution. I don't like this idea
but can see the sense in what he
is saying and I don't know how
to reply.’

THE PHILOSOPHER'S REPLY:

Many hold that human beings are simply a result of Darwinian
Natural Selection and the survival of the fittest. If this is the
case, then there is no reason to suppose that the human race
is the end-point of evolution. It certainly is the high point of
evolution so far, but something else with a greater capacity
for survival may come to dominate and human beings will be
seen as yet one more step in the evolutionary process which
may eventually be selected out and eliminated. It could easily
be that unchecked global warming and climate change or even

nuclear war could accelerate this process. It is also possible, however, that the creation of advanced artificial intelligence, possibly incorporating aspects of human biology, may be the future.

Oxford University has a 'Centre for Humanity Institute' which brings together philosophers, biologists and others to look at where the human race goes next. Already humans can manipulate the genome and the discovery of CrispR (an incredible gene editing tool which allows genes to be inserted or removed from a human or animal embryo) and genetic selection of embryos through Pre-Implantation Genetic Diagnosis have opened up the possibility of altering and 'improving' (whatever that means) future human babies. 'Transhumanism' is the new discipline which looks at the possibilities of going beyond the human. Elon Musk, to whom you referred, is a billionaire and head of SpaceX and Tesla, but also of a company called Neuralink which is looking at, basically, the possibility of integrating the equivalent of a SIM from a smart phone into human brains so that all the knowledge of the internet would immediately be available without the tedious business of learning. Research on these areas is developing rapidly but is still in its infancy.

Many may feel a natural repugnance to accept that human beings are simply one step in a developing evolutionary process but the dinosaurs, if they could have thought rationally, would probably have felt the same.

A religious perspective on life is likely to reject such moves and to insist that human beings have been created by God and it is wrong to interfere with what God has created (except to cure diseases). Christianity teaches that human beings are the pinnacle of God's creation and are in a different category to any animal. Human beings have freedom and are immortal. No other creature has these qualities. It is obvious there are different perspectives on this issue, but it seems inevitable that there will be crosses produced between biological humans and artificial intelligence. Already computer storage is beginning to be used based on DNA so the boundaries between physics and biology are becoming blurred. Whether this is right or not will depend on what you believe about the status of human beings in the universe, about whether natural selection can provide a complete understanding of what it means to be human and, in the final analysis the most fundamental question of all – whether you believe in a Reality that underpins the whole of creation and which cares about the position of human beings. This reality may be what religious people call God.

Dr Stefan Sorgner

Chair of the Department of History and Humanities, John Cabot University, Rome, Italy, Director of the Beyond Humanism Network

We are undoubtedly advanced animals. The last common ancestor of great apes and human beings existed 6 million years ago. Homo sapiens came into existence about 400,000 years ago. Where will we be in another 400,000 or 6 million years? We might have evolved further - and implanted chips and gene technologies will most likely influence evolutionary processes. As a species, we will either develop further or we will die out. However, does our being advanced animals or our evolutionary future being affected by chip implantation mean that there is no meaning in life?

What makes life meaningful? Our actions making a difference to us personally beyond this life, as they would in a personal afterlife where our behaviour on earth influences what happens to us after death? I must say that we do not have any strong reason for holding that there is a realm into which we enter after we will have died. Yet, having the possibility to enhance evolution does not have any relevance concerning the question whether there is a personal afterlife or not. No one can exclude the possibility of there being a personal afterlife. We could be both evolved animals and possess a divine spark. No one can rule out this option either. Please doubt anyone who makes any other claim.

Even if there is no personal afterlife, our actions could make a difference to us personally beyond this life and life could still be meaningful. If energy is all there is and energy is always governed by the same fundamental laws, then in a finite universe there must be a state in which all possible energetic shapes will have occurred. Yet, if the universe is finite, it must be true both that all possible energetic shapes have already occurred in the past at a certain moment and that they must recur identically in the future. Hence, everything that has happened in the past must recur again and again and again. This also applies to us; each one of us will have to live their lives repeatedly in an identical manner. So, each of our actions has a personal relevance for us that transcends this life ... because we are destined to repeat this same action again and again in the future. Each act is, therefore, ultimately meaningful ... even if there is no personal afterlife in an immaterial world separate from the one around us.

Still, what if the fundamental laws we observe now do not apply in other parts of the universe? Then, eternal recurrence of all our actions might not be plausible concept of meaning. It is this openness to contingencies which also demands the avoidance of directly being violent against others, as the judgement of others might be more appropriate than your own.

Are these reflections making any sense to you? I am curious to hearing how these reflections resonate with your thinking.

HOW DO I MAKE SENSE OF RELATIONSHIPS WITH THE WIDER COMMUNITY?

22.

'My sister and I raised £1695 for the Salvation Army by organising a charity event in our school because we were so worried about the number of children who don't have Christmas presents or even food. Why do most adults not care or do anything?'

THE PHILOSOPHEr'S rePLY:

Almost everyone recognises that they should do more to help those less fortunate than themselves but, sadly, all too few people take this seriously. They will often give a small amount to charity when it does not inconvenience them and perhaps because it makes them feel good but that is about all. Of course, today, people pay taxes and some of these taxes are used to assist people who are poor and vulnerable although the percentage varies in different societies. The financial 'safety net' which aims to protect those who are poorest and most vulnerable tends to be more generous in Europe than in the United States and in many countries even a basic level of protection against homelessness, long term illness, unemployment or retirement barely exists. In Britain the government has cut the amount given in overseas aid from 0.7 per cent of GDP to 0.5 per cent and this aid is going to in future be channelled in ways which promote the government's interests.

Peter Singer is an atheist philosopher (see Question 13) yet he gives 20 per cent of his income away to charitable causes and argues that this should be an absolute minimum. He seeks to live simply by spending as little as possible on himself and he maintains that if one spends money on luxuries which one does not really need when one knows that millions in the world and in one's own country are in desperate poverty this is morally wrong. A failure to act is, he claims, an ethical failure. Very few religious people give anything like 10 per cent let alone 20 per cent to charity. In the United States about 2 per cent of the total value of the economy is given to charities by individuals and the largest share of these donations go to religious charities – but only a part of this goes to the poor.

Jesus told the story of the sheep and the goats when he was asked who would go to heaven. He did not say that those who went to Church would achieve salvation but that those who found him in the poor, the weak, the vulnerable, those in prison, those in hospital would enter his kingdom. In many ways his message was very similar to that of the atheist Peter Singer although he would differ strongly from Singer about the sanctity of human life and about the possibility of life after death.

The lack of compassion shown by many people is due to several reasons. First, there is what is called 'compassion fatigue' – the feeling that so many people suffer from war, famine, poverty, etc. that what little an individual could do would be almost meaningless. Secondly, there is a considerable amount of corruption in some countries and some individuals feel that money given to some charities will sometimes be misused. Thirdly, and perhaps most importantly, people do not see the human face of those who suffer. If it were their next door neighbour, they might be more inclined to help, but when it is someone on the other side of the world (maybe with a different religion, skin colour or sexual orientation) they find it easy to ignore their need.

You obviously did something with the Salvation Army that made a difference. If more people would do the same, not just on a one-off basis but continually, the world could be a much better and happier place. Sadly, too few people respond.

Dr Tim Macnaught
Former Head of Religious Studies, Anglican Grammar Schools, Melbourne

The inscription on a memorial window in an old Canberra church reads, 'He never turned his face from a poor man', quoting some famous advice in the biblical story of Tobias which added the promise: 'and the face of God won't be turned away from you.' The duty (and blessing) of sharing our wealth has ancient roots in the Jewish tradition. Even a poor person had to give something to another person, because it was recognised there is more dignity in giving than in receiving. Laws on 'tithing' required setting aside for God a tenth or more of one's produce to give thanks — recognising that everything ultimately belongs to God, so a portion should be given back. This carried over into Christian advice such as 'God loves a cheerful giver'.

One of the pillars of Islam, too, is to give from our surplus to the needy. Jesus had some tough warnings about clinging to wealth (e.g., the story of the rich man and Lazarus.) One of the worst things about money-making is that it can become like an addiction, something the rich think about day and night. And they never feel they have enough. Because they are stingy, they are never happy. (I remember as a child asking my grandmother why her friends who came to visit in Rolls Royces looked so miserable. 'Well, darling,' she said, 'at least they're miserable in comfort!')

Millions in so-called rich countries, as you know, depend on charity to get by. Others have decent jobs, houses and cars but struggle to pay off their loans and have nothing left over to give away. Still, many do care and give generously. In my country, Australia, there are 56,000 registered charities that flourish on donations. 'Crowd funding' via social media is huge. For instance, a group of surfers raised $18,000 in a few days to Medivac home an injured mate from Bali. During the terrible 2020 bushfires, a koala hospital in NSW appealed for $50,000 emergency assistance to treat badly burnt animals and raised over $2,000,000 in a few days.

Then there are the big-time philanthropists like Bill Gates who donate millions to causes such as eliminating diseases like polio or malaria. Or have you heard of the toilet paper outfit with the cheeky name Who Gives a Crap? They dedicate half their profits to building toilets in poor countries. And there is a young Australian couple who are promising to give away most of the A$16 billion they have made recently from their graphic design software (Canva). They see themselves not as billionaires but as 'custodians' of wealth with which 'to do good in the world'. What you are saying, I think, is that we need more people like them — and everyone else just to do their bit, as you have, for a better world.

DR TOMMY LYNCH
Reader in Political Theology, University of Chichester

IMAGINE YOU HAVE A GLASS OF WATER,
AND EACH DROP OF WATER IN THAT GLASS
IS THE ATTENTION YOU CAN PAY TO SOMETHING.

If most people—many of whom we think are 'good people'— were more generous with their time or money the world would be a better place. I think the answer goes beyond just not caring. There are two parts to understanding this problem: individuals and society.

For individuals, each person is limited in the number of things that they can really care about. Imagine you have a glass of water, and each drop of water in that glass is the attention you can pay to something: friends, pets, your job, world events, social media, what you are going to cook for dinner, etc. Each thing gets given a certain number of drops until the glass is dry.

For most people, there are things that seem to need more attention than others. Parents spend a lot of their drops of attention on their children and their needs. When we get to things that are not part of our day-to-day life, they usually get fewer drops. Most people agree climate change is a worrying problem, but how much attention are they really devoting to it?

One reason that people devote more attention to their children than to these big problems, is that their children respond to attention. Likewise, if you stop paying attention to your job there are consequences. There may be consequences to paying less attention to big problems, but those are in the distant future.

Poverty and inequality are examples of these big problems. Unless you are experiencing poverty and inequality, they feel removed from day-to-day life. It is no secret that there are many people who struggle to have the things they need, but any given individual only has so many drops of attention. When something changes—when a kind person points out that children need Christmas presents—that problem goes from a big, far away issue, to being closer and more personal. When Christmas is over, those drops are shifted away from the needs of people who are struggling, back to work and what you need to buy at the supermarket.

Not everyone lives this way. There are people who, for a variety of reasons, pay attention to these big problems. There are also those who devote their attention to people that they make part of their day-to-day life: either by volunteering or working at jobs that help people. That work can often feel defeating, though; it seems like the drops of attention are not making much of a difference.

Here is where society comes in. The nineteenth-century German philosopher G. W. F. Hegel argues that a society that needs charity is a flawed society. It is good for people to be generous and charitable, but it is bad for people to need generosity and charity. It is important to ask why people do not pay more attention to people in need and we can be more careful about where we put our drops of attention, but it is also important to ask why there are people in need in the first place.

23.

'If the aim of life to be happy should we not put old people out of their misery if they are in pain and want to die?'

THE PHILOSOPHEr'S rePLY:

Old age can, indeed, be burdensome. People are living longer and longer but sometimes the quality of their lives can be poor. Arthritis, Alzheimer's, Parkinson's, Huntington's, Dementia and similar diseases are increasingly common; incontinence can lead to a loss of dignity and some people cannot eat and have to be fed through tubes. Doctors are getting better and better at relieving pain but palliative care (largely pain relief) cannot always overcome all pain as one gets to the final stages of life. All these factors have led many to argue that what matters is 'Quality of Life' and the religious idea of 'Sanctity of Life' is an outmoded notion. Peter Singer argues for this position (see Question 13). Although, however, this certainly has attractions it also suffers from real dangers – for instance Singer is willing to argue for the killing of babies up to a month old as their quality of life would be poor. Many disabled children and adults nevertheless have a wonderful quality of life. Children with Down's syndrome are a good example as, in spite of their severe disadvantages, they are often full of joy which they communicate to others.

Few doctors want to turn from being healthcare providers to being agents of death – even if this is at the request of the person who is terminally ill. Sadly, in today's society we tend not to value the wisdom of old people in the way that was normal in the past and is still the case in many societies. Britain has a wonderful hospice movement which seeks to make the final stage of life as happy and pain free as possible. Certainly in answer to your question euthanasia and assisted suicide should only be considered if this is really what the person concerned wants and if it is subject to stringent safeguards – however even if these are in place, abandoning the principle of the Sanctity of human life may be too high a price to pay as it may open a slippery slope which undermines the value of the older generation and, more widely, the preciousness of human life.

THE RT HON THE LORD WALLACE OF TANKERNESS KC
Moderator, Church of Scotland

I have chosen this question because it is topical, with legislation on assisted dying currently before both the House of Lords and the Scottish Parliament. But firstly, I would query the premise of the question. Is the aim of life to be 'happy'? In the Presbyterian tradition in which I was brought up, we were taught that the chief aim of life is 'to glorify God and enjoy Him forever'. 'Glorify' meaning to worship and 'enjoy Him forever' can be understood as enjoying fruits of faith such as forgiveness or guidance or love. The other difficulty I have is how we assess happiness. Each of us is an individual and almost certainly will have a different idea of what it means to be happy. This poses the fundamental issue as to who is to judge whether someone is happy or not, before taking such drastic action as 'putting someone out of their misery'. But even if the question is reframed to allow for the possibility that someone is asking for help to take their own life, I still have very serious misgivings.

As a Christian, I recognise that the importance of caring, including care for those approaching the end of their lives. My faith causes me to have several concerns around the principle of assisted dying: the application of the law in practice, and the effect which any change in the law may have on the way in which society views those of our fellow citizens in need of care, and who are often the weak, vulnerable, and voiceless. There is a very strong societal view on the importance of the protection of life; to move away from this would involve much more than a simple amendment of the law. Instead, it would represent a significant change in how society regards those in our communities who are vulnerable, from which there would be no return. This could have profound effects - not just on elderly people in pain, but also on those with disabilities, and on those who are unable to speak up to protect themselves. While proposed legislation seeks to include safeguards against misappropriation of assisted dying, the experience in other countries where attempts have been made to frame and apply safeguards around it suggests that assisted dying is fraught with difficulty.

The end of a person's life involves not simply the moment of their death, but also the way in which they experience their final days and weeks. Our decisions and actions have effects on others. Life is lived and death experienced as part of community and society. Of course, there should be the provision of proper palliative care *[end of life care]*, but changing the law to allow the possibility of being able to put elderly people out of their misery is a Rubicon I do not wish to cross.

DR TIM MACNAUGHT

Former Head of Religious Studies, Anglican Grammar Schools, Melbourne

The happiest old people I know don't really aim to be happy: they're happy because they live well, give generously of their time and money, and have loving relationships. 'Okay,' you might say, 'but when their health fails and they find themselves in terrible pain night and day, wouldn't it be kinder to put them out of their misery or at least help them take their own life ('assisted suicide')? We put down our beloved pets and horses when they are 'past it', why not humans?'

The arguments for euthanasia are fast winning over lawmakers around the world. Many are no longer convinced by the traditional view that the life-force is sacred, a share in God's own life; they see life as a part of the body which we own and can treat like any other bit of property. 'We have a right to die', they say, and that some lives are just not worth living.

The first euthanasia laws were introduced by Hitler in October 1939 when he had doctors kill people the Nazis saw as 'unworthy of living' or 'parasites' on state welfare: the incurably ill, the disabled, the insane, and frail elderly. The Nazis set up efficient killing centres with poison gas chambers to murder 200,000 people before and during the war. They expanded these into the Holocaust program to exterminate millions of Jews.

Supporters of euthanasia hate any mention of the Nazis, but they do share the basic idea that some lives are not worth living and that we have a right to end them or at least allow doctors to assist sufferers to kill themselves. Religious traditions protest that the life force, like personal dignity or the environment, is 'sacred' or 'sacrosanct' meaning not ours to do with as we wish. The wisdom of the ages has taught us not to treat created life as our personal possession.

Human decisions like the introduction of euthanasia often have unintended consequences, unpleasant results no one expected. To legalise dying is to make life itself disposable, and to put pressure on the seriously ill not to be a burden to their carers. Generally, to get euthanasia laws through parliament, there are strict conditions to limit their use. But inevitably, as we have seen in the Netherlands and Belgium, agitation soon mounts to extend euthanasia to, say, younger people in no danger of dying but whose lives are miserable and not seen by them or their families as worth living.

Doctors have excellent drugs to manage pain and discomfort as part of 'palliative care' programs that surround the dying (and their families) with emotional and spiritual support and accompany the person to their last breath. These medications can cause a gradual loss of consciousness (and maybe shorten life) but still allow a more natural and often quite peaceful death. Even with pain, families report that those final days and hours can be a very significant and precious time for all.

24.

‘Cars rust and get old. Why do adults get so excited buying a new one?’

THE PHILOSOPHER'S REPLY:

When someone buys a car they are not simply buying a car. They are buying a means of transport, a lifestyle choice, comfort, perhaps safety and, sometimes most important, a mark of their success and something that displays this success to others. Almost all cars have four wheels, a steering wheel, brakes and an engine. Almost every modern car has many safety features ranging from safety belts, air bags, emergency braking, perhaps collision avoidance technology and many others. The difference, in practical terms, between a Nissan Micra and a top of the range Mercedes Benz, BMW, Lexus, Porsche, Volvo or similar high end car is relatively small. A Porsche may cost ten times as much as a small car but there is certainly not ten times the inherent value. What the top end car does is to affirm the status of the person buying or driving it, it evokes admiration from neighbours and colleagues, it shows the social status of the person (arriving at a party in a Porsche will have a different impact than arriving in a Fiat). So the person buying a new car (whether this is actually new or a second hand car that is new to the person buying it) provides a sense of wellbeing and worth as well as status both in the eyes of many others but, more important, in the eyes of the driver and his or her family.

When Pope Francis become Pope he was given a 20-year-old Fiat to drive which had been used by an old priest and the Pope uses this regularly. When he visited President Obama in the White House he arrived not in a Cadillac, a Buick, a Rolls Royce or a Mercedes but in a Fiat. Obama, prior to becoming President, drove several Fords and a Jeep. The choice of car is an indication of priorities. A modest car may be all that a person can afford but it can also indicate that all that was sought was an effective means of transport. Everything else is trivial.

Fran Horner
International tax lawyer, Washington, USA

What wonderful questions you have. Let me say right off that I don't know the answers, and you should not treat what I say as truth. The only true thing I can say here is that your observation is correct: Adults do get excited about buying a new car. Truth is like that – it is most solid when it simply describes what you see. As to the Why - well, that's a different matter entirely. The Why is a matter of opinion, especially when it comes to matters of the spirit and heart. Opinions can reflect experience and wisdom, so take it all in, listen, consider, and then make up your own minds – which could change as the years pass.

Anyway, here's what I think: we are beings bound by time, so each moment is to be valued for the good it conveys. While this moment's goodness can fade or diminish or vanish completely in a second or a week or a year, it makes its mark anyway. It leaves an impression that echoes forward through time and maybe even backwards. One of my favourite philosopher-saints, Edith Stein, thought that our good works today could even somehow erase evil that happened years ago. I tend to agree with her. It really doesn't matter that the car might be wrecked in the next moment. Here and now, it is something to behold.

Why do we love shiny new things like cars? Maybe it's because they reflect in a single item the history and ingenuity of the human person, the talent of the designer, the care of the one who polished and finished, the gift of inventiveness and creation that we received from God. How could we not be excited by such a thing, my goodness! When we purchase a car, we know it will accompany us for some years, and age like us, bearing the marks of good times and bad. It is both evidence and promise of the human spirit.

Just because something gets old and wears out does not really diminish its value, at least not to the heart. Think about your Godmother Wendy. She is getting older, and she may feel her bones are a little bit rusty. Do you love her any less? I don't know about you, but my love for her has only grown. She was great when she was shiny and new, but I like her even better now. She has the beauty of a life well lived and her few wrinkles are treasures. I suppose it is the same for cars: Many people love their old cars just as much as when they were new.

25.

'Most British prime ministers and even the Archbishop of Canterbury went to the same very expensive school while my parents can only send us to a state school with big class sizes. Is this fair or right?'

EVEN THE ARCHBISHOP OF
CANTERBURY
WENT TO THE SAME VERY
EXPENSIVE SCHOOL

THE PHILOSOPHER'S REPLY:

It is not fair or right that some people can afford the most exceptional education that will confer privilege, power, wealth and contacts on their children merely because their parents have the very substantial financial resources that an independent, private education often (not always) brings. There is little question that the best jobs in the law, in politics, in business, in broadcasting and in almost every field frequently go to independently educated students and there seems no way to rationally justify this.

Parents will always want 'the best' for their children and for most parents this is defined in terms of success. Parents are willing to sacrifice a great deal to achieve this success and many children of wealthy parents are thereby given the gift of small class sizes and excellent facilities. Care for one's offspring is deeply ingrained in all animals and also humans.

Philippa Foot, in the 1960s, developed what has become known as 'The Trolley Problem'. A variation on this might be as follows. Imagine you are standing next to a railway line by some points. There is a runaway train whose brakes have failed coming fast down a hill. There is no way of stopping it. Directly on the line just past where you are standing are ten refugees in a container on the line. They will inevitably be killed by the oncoming train. There is a chance, however. You can change the points and the train will be diverted onto a track on which your mother is sunbathing. She is deaf and won't hear the train. What would you do?

Most people would let the refugees be killed. But why? On what basis do you prefer to kill ten innocent people (which is what will happen if you do nothing) rather than killing your mother? There seems no answer to this. The parallel, of course, is with education – why spend up to £400,000 or more on your own children when the same sum of money would transform the lives of many children living in poverty in rural Africa?

Some countries such as France have sought to avoid the problem of independent education, but the rich and powerful will always seek to find a way to confer advantage on their offspring. This is a perfectly natural, human reaction but it is a position that cannot be rationally justified. The great German philosopher Immanuel Kant argued that every person is of equal value and is of irreducible worth. If this is accepted (as most declarations about human rights affirm) then the consequences must be that buying privilege cannot be justified.

In England the class system is perpetuated by independent schools which are generally given charitable status even though their activities principally benefit the wealthy. Eton, the school to which you implicitly refer in your question, costs about £45,000 per year. A child who is there for five years will therefore cost his parents about £240,000 with extras. This has to be paid out of after tax income – assuming a 40 per cent rate of tax the parents would have to earn £400,000 just to pay for school fees. In addition they will have paid for junior school education and probably for University – so they would have to earn about £700,000 just to finance one child's education. Most such schools will make some small effort to show that they do some very limited charity work to 'tick boxes' required by the charity commissioners, but few governments seek to limit the influence of independent schools – possibly because many politicians send their children to these institutions. It is not hard to imagine what could be achieved in Africa or parts of South America or Southeast Asia if £700,000 was devoted to providing high quality schooling there,

Some exceptional people do, of course, make it through the state funded education to become very successful and some universities in some countries make an effort to take into account the greater difficulties faced by state educated students, but your general point is a perfectly fair and reasonable one. Perhaps your parents do not have the wealth to provide the opportunities that a very few others have – although hopefully they may try to compensate for this in other ways.

Fran Horner
International tax lawyer, Washington, USA

I fear you may be falling into the trap of believing that something that costs more or is exclusive is necessarily better. I haven't experienced that in my life. There are colours and contours and special gifts to each expression of life. A young girl may miss out the individual attention and exceptional teachers the Prime Minister had, but in her large ordinary state school, she may be surrounded by good lifelong friends, and be taught by people who know the challenges and burdens of life, who have the depth and heart that comes from struggle. Who is to say which is best?

Each person is able to express a dimension of God that no one else has, because each person is unique. If you spend your whole life trying to be the same as others, God on earth will never be whole. It is our differences that are the gift. Just look at yourselves! It is in our diversity that we find strength, and beauty and truth. No one person can capture the truth on their own.

So when you ask whether it is fair that not everyone is treated the same, I say: resist the idea that we should all be treated the same. Work to give everyone opportunity and ensure human rights. But never embrace homogeneity *[effectively making everyone the same]*. That's a big word, though you probably understand it. It's like when they blend cream into milk to make it all the same. If we were a homogeneous culture, we'd only value skin of one colour. We'd have no special indigenous foods, we'd all think the same – or be punished for our differences. How horrible that would be.

Honestly, the best parts of my life did not come from my elite experiences. I remember when I was in Paris leading a choir that was mostly filled with poor laborers, who cleaned houses for the rich. They were among the best people I have ever known. Their faith was strong and shone through their eyes. They cared for one another and all people. They were happy and free. It is important to step back and get some perspective on what is truly valuable in a human life. And I can tell you right now: that has nothing to do with how expensive or elite your school is. You know I am right.

26.

‘We did a school project on the Victorians including Victorian gaols and I visited a Victorian prison. We look back now and think how terribly the Victorians treated their prisoners but I wonder whether our children will look back on today and wonder the same about today's prisons? I am not sure what people today think prisons are for?’

THE PHILOSOPHER'S REPLY:

It is true, as your question implies, that prison conditions match the society in which they develop. There are various reasons for this. Those in prison can be easily forgotten as people generally feel that inmates are in prison due to their own fault, that they deserve to be punished and that their presence in prison safeguards society. All these assumptions can be challenged. The re-offending rate of people leaving

I AM NOT SURE WHAT PEOPLE
TODAY THINK PRISONS ARE FOR?

prisons is high. They often cannot get employment; their relationships may have been destroyed by their time in prison and they may have limited or no financial resources or skills. The lack of skills is particularly important as the amount spent on education of prisoners has, in most Western countries, been cut considerably in the last twenty years.

The issue of prison sentences being what the prisoners deserve is a complex one. In some cases this is undoubtedly true but if one takes time to understand individual prisoners' stories, the situation is often far more complex. There are many reasons why people commit crimes including psychiatric disorders, too few resources to help people with these disorders, the breakdown of relationships, a family record of crime, a history of drug use and sometimes sheer desperation to find the means to meet basic needs, such as to feed and clothe their families. There is also increasing evidence that there may be genetic factors at play – for instance, there is evidence both from Sweden and New Zealand that some individuals carry genes that make it more likely that they will become violent.

The second major factor is financial. Western governments face increasing financial pressure due to the cost of old age care, the need for roads, railways, power stations, social care, pensions, defence and education spending, as well as competitive pressures from countries such as China, India, Vietnam and Cambodia, make it difficult for some Western companies to compete. Faced with these pressures, politicians find it easy to neglect the needs of prisoners and to recognise that a major change of attitude is required. More effort needs to be put into education, rehabilitation and seeing the human face of those in prison. This will, however, only happen when ordinary people recognise that prison conditions are unacceptable and politicians are forced to review their priorities.

Cardinal John Dew
Archbishop of Wellington, New Zealand

Victorian prisons were terrible places, damp, over-crowded and unhealthy, as I am sure you saw when you visited one. I think the worst aspect of those prisons was that you could be there for a very minor offence, or because you were so poor you stole food. Even children were not spared going to prison.

Your question about what people think prisons are for tells me you have made the connection between our society and the type of prisons we have, which is a very important insight. Our prisons reflect how people think about those who offend. When people think offenders should be punished and deterred from further offending, they want prisons to be as unpleasant as possible. More extreme calls for harsh imprisonment are really about revenge.

Many politicians who make decisions about the law and the prison system respond to how society sees the offenders. These politicians want to win at the next election. We know now that most prisoners have problems with addictions, mental health, and damaging family relationships. If they did not succeed at school, they may have dropped out without the skills needed for employment.

When people understand the disadvantages and difficulties many prisoners have had in their lives, they are more likely to favour an approach to crime which focusses on repairing the harm the prisoner has done and helping them to change their lives. We want the prisoner to return to society with the relationship skills to relate well to family and friends, and the employment skills to stay away from crime.

Some prisoners – only a small part of the prison population – are so dangerous and unable or unwilling to change that they must be kept in a secure environment to protect other people. But they are very few, and even they should live in conditions that recognize they are human beings.

In the early 1990s Norway began to rebuild its prison system to focus on the rehabilitation and healing of the people in its care. Their system is based on a strong belief in the dignity and humanness of each person. Prisoners are treated with respect, helped to study, they learn relationship skills and do useful work. They live within a supportive community where prison officers are more like mentors or coaches. The goal is to prepare the prisoner for life outside the prison, and this is helped by a key principle, that 'during the serving of a sentence, life inside will resemble life outside as much as possible'. Prisons are more like villages, and prisoners have a lot of freedom. There is now a lot of evidence that this approach helps prisoners not to re-offend.

I think future generations may well wonder why prisoners were treated so harshly in many countries in the twenty-first century. But they may also look at Norway and a few other countries and see a time of transition from punishment and deterrence to rehabilitation and healing. If you ever have the opportunity to advocate for this change then you will be doing a great service to the community.

THE RT REVD RACHEL TREWEEK
Bishop of Gloucester, Anglican bishop responsible for prisons

If you ask people what prisons are for you will probably get a range of answers: They are there to keep our communities safe by locking away people who harm other people; they are there to punish people and ensure that those who have committed crime are deprived of their freedom and suffer the consequences of their behaviour; and they are there to rehabilitate people and enable them to change their attitudes and behaviour. I would say that all of these are true to varying degrees yet as a Christian and as the Anglican Bishop for Prisons in England and Wales, I want to work for a prison system which keeps relationship, dignity, and the fulfilling of potential at its heart, yet at the same time never dismissing the seriousness of wrongdoing or failing to recognise the pain of victims of crime and the impact on communities.

There is a populist view that our streets and communities will be safer and better if all those who commit crimes are given longer sentences and punished more harshly, and that furthermore it will deter people from committing crime if they recognise what the consequences might be. I disagree and there is no evidence to show that longer prison sentences deter people from committing crime, or that someone is more likely to be reformed and less likely to reoffend.

While there are people who commit dreadful and evil

crimes and who need to be kept locked up in order to keep people safe, I also believe that there are many people behind bars for whom prison is not the right place to bring about change and reduce reoffending. These people are not dangerous to the public, and while there is a need to face up to their wrongdoing there is also a need to address some of the key underlying factors which have brought them to this place, and thus enable them to refrain from re-offending and to contribute positively to their communities.

A major problem, as I see it, is that the prison system is not designed to engage with the underlying trauma in people's own personal stories and is not able to cope with treating each offender as a unique individual. Of course, none of this is to ignore a victim's pain and suffering, and a good system needs to be able to confront each offender with the impact of their crime.

We need a system that can work effectively with more offenders in a community setting rather than sentencing them to prison. This provision allows people to be part of groups which enable the learning of new patterns of behaviour while at the same time addressing issues such as addictions and building self-esteem through strong relationships with people such as key workers, who value them and help address their stories. The evidence is that this holistic all-round approach reduces offending, often enables families to stay together, and builds stronger communities in the long term. Working with more offenders in community settings rather than prison will reduce overcrowding in our prisons as well as saving vast amounts of money.

Finally, in asking what prisons are for we need to be asking some even bigger questions about how we work at building a society which prevents people from engaging in criminal activity in the first place.

27.

> ❝Why do people spend so much time watching football, cookery and gardening programmes on television when they could be out doing something?❞

THE PHILOSOPHER'S REPLY:

For some, the activities you mention are enjoyable. They help to pass the time, are interesting and in a way engaging. In some cases, they are educational. Many people spend a huge percentage of their lives either watching televisions or on their mobile phones. In many relationships today people spend more time and energy on their mobile phones or watching television than engaging with another human being. While, however, some may find such activities enjoyable there is another, perhaps more cynical but perhaps more accurate, way of looking at these activities and that is to regard them as distractions from the real point of being alive.

Many people suffer from depression and there are many reasons which may cause this dreadful condition. There is evidence, although it is not yet conclusive, that some forms of depression may be genetic. Most forms of depression are due to many other possible factors. To list them all would take a book, but they can range from abuse or neglect as a child, a lack of love, being betrayed in a relationship, a sense of being worthless or being a failure, loss of a job, house or material wealth, and so on. Sometimes depression, particularly in teenagers, can lead to self-harm – the individual inflicts physical pain on themselves to distract them from the emotional pain of being alive. Sometimes depression can lead to taking drugs or becoming addicted to alcohol – again as a way of escaping from a sense of hopelessness. However, all these are extreme, albeit tragic, cases and have no direct bearing on your question.

Most people do not suffer from any form of what might be described as depression in psycho-analytic terms. Nevertheless, for many people life can be lonely and without any real purpose or point – they therefore need distractions to avoid confronting what, for some, is the real pain of existence. Watching television can provide precisely the distraction that people may need. For some older people who are alone, television may provide a sense of 'company' and, again, a distraction. The Danish philosopher Søren Kierkegaard argued that most people live lives of quiet despair. Even if this is not the case, at the end of a long day many may simply be tired and want to 'switch off'.

I would suggest, therefore, that for individuals such as you suggest who spend, in your words, 'so much time' watching television this can be seen as a distraction from the serious business of being alive. It passes the time and appears harmless. I say 'appears' as if life has some other purpose than pleasure or distraction then devoting large amounts of time to television can be a real distraction from the serious business of living life and standing up for those who are vulnerable, lonely, hungry or in need. My solution? Forget yourself and engage with others, worry more about others than you do about yourself. Life demands more than existing. Charles Mackay's poem expresses it well:

You have no enemies you say?
Alas my friend the boast is poor,
He who has mingled in the fray
of duty that the brave endure
Must have made foes! If you have none,
Small is the work that you have done.
You've hit no traitor on the hip,
You dashed no cup from perjured lip,
You've never turned the wrong to right
You've been a coward in the fight.

Don't worry about questions of meaning – engage with the world. Help others in as many practical ways as possible even if these are small: Stand up for Truth and Justice: Even a smile or a brief comment on a walk can change a person's day.

Dr Louise Nelstrop

Director of Studies, Margaret Beaufort Institute, Cambridge

Without doing a lot of market research it would be very difficult to give a definite answer to this question. The answer also won't be the same for everyone. One professional footballer reported watching inspiring clips to motivate himself before a game. But in terms of people who are mostly just watching, a study found that the 'fear of missing out' is a major factor that governs why people binge watch TV or tune in to watch major sporting events. People are afraid that they are missing something good that others are getting access to. The level of excitement that is generated by watching a sport like football also keeps viewers hooked, meaning that they don't switch channels or go off and do something else. Viewers are more likely to watch football on TV if there is the possibility of seeing superstars, if the team plays to a high standard and especially if they are playing good opposition, and the outcome is uncertain. If they didn't watch, they could miss out on all this. Adolescents are more likely to spend a lot of time in front of the TV but interestingly their parents are worried that their children are missing out on opportunities that they never had when they were young. So, the fear of missing out also plays a factor in parents' concerns that children should get out and do things instead of just watching TV!

Watching football on TV is often done for reasons of entertainment. However, it's clear that people don't watch cookery or gardening shows simply to be entertained in the comfort of their own homes. Cookery and gardening shows both count as what is called 'lifestyle television'. This means that they show us, potentially, what our lifestyle ought to be like. Based on the kinds of questions that viewers send in, it's clear that viewers are really interested in food and gardening and like having the opportunity to learn about them from experts. Since viewers' questions often get answered live on air, this also creates a feeling of community with the pleasure of cooking, for example, as its focus. Lifestyle television shows also are not watched in absolute opposition to getting out and doing things. It's more complicated than this. Watching cookery shows has been linked to helping people avoid food-related hygiene problems in their own kitchens. However, a recent book suggests the link with action can also be worrying where viewers are encouraged to adopt middle class values that they can't afford. A string of thefts was linked to gardening shows that suggested people put down a particular kind of paving for example. The reasons that motivate people to watch these kinds of shows therefore varies. Whether the effect of watching rather than just doing is good for us is a different question!

28.

'Why does the news spend so much time on politics and why do adults get so angry with people who disagree with them about politics?'

THE PHILOSOPHER'S REPLY:

Politics matters. The way a country is governed, its relationships with the outside world, the way that old and vulnerable people are cared for, how medical cover is provided, the maintenance of infrastructure (roads, railways, electricity, gas and water supplies), defence needs, what is legal and what is not (including the age of sexual consent, abortion, divorce, euthanasia, treatment of children), the conduct of business, taxation policy and almost every aspect of life are covered by politics. People have strong views about all these issues and since the issues are determined in political discussion it is not surprising that strong views are held about politics as well.

When strong views are challenged, people get angry. Often political views are tied into culture and rejecting the culture and associated political views of one's family and friends can lead to disagreement which can rapidly becoming heated. In some countries, political discussion is not allowed (China,

Russia, Myanmar, North Korea and many others) although even in these countries discussion, although suppressed, continues beneath the surface. In supposed democracies, political loyalties are sometimes almost tribal. In the United States people often identify as Democrat or Republican and see the world through the eyes of media which support their own party while demonising opposing views.

It is not hard, therefore, to understand why politics generates strong emotions. This should not, however, be the case. It should be possible to argue for a political position whilst identifying the weakness of one's own views and the strengths of views with which one disagrees. This is why a training in philosophy is so important for good education as philosophy teaches (or should teach) the importance of a search of truth and putting forward arguments rather than just opinions to support any view that is held.

Philosophy should also teach people that their own views may be mistaken. A good philosopher will always be pleased to be shown the error of his or her own position and should be willing to challenge and sometimes reject her or his own most cherished assumptions. Too few educational systems value philosophy and, therefore, emotion rather than good argument tends to dominate much political debate coupled, sadly, with a search for power by politicians who recognise that only when they have power will they be able to implement their ideas. Increasingly, some politicians will sometimes compromise truth in favour of gaining power.

THE RT HON THE LORD WALLACE OF TANKERNESS KC
Moderator, Church of Scotland

May I answer this not only as Moderator of the General Assembly of the Church of Scotland, but as someone who has spent most of my adult life in politics? From time immemorial, politics in one form or another has shaped societies and how we live our lives. In modern times, the reach of politics is immense: education, health, social care, what we pay in taxes, how society supports the vulnerable – at home and abroad, transport links, the environment, climate change, relations between countries, how we are defended, how we are protected, when we can legally marry, what constitutes a legal sale of property, how the state is organised … I could go on. These are just some examples of aspects of life which are determined by political decisions. Just think of how decisions by politicians affected us all during the pandemic, when governments took powers unprecedented out of wartime. Given the reach of politics into so many of the things we do, it is not surprising that a considerable amount of news time is given to reporting and discussing it. I think there are two main reasons why this is important. First, people need to know what is happening, especially if affects their lives. Secondly, in a democracy, where we get to choose which politicians govern, it is vital that people have the information on which they can make their choice. I believe that information is the currency of a properly functioning democracy. In turn, that places a responsibility on broadcasters to impart news and question politicians in a way which is impartial and informative.

Because political decisions are so pervasive, it is not surprising that they evoke passions. People inevitably have different views and that is generally healthy. It would be dull

– and dangerous – if, as under some totalitarian regimes *[governments which reject any opinion or view other than their own and impose this on the population of their countries – examples include North Korea and Russia]*, everyone was obliged to hold the same opinion. However, that does not justify anger. People should express their views in ways which do not provoke anger. In turn, it is important for politicians in Parliament as well as for customers in pubs or families around the meal table to respect the views of others. For most of my lifetime, that has generally been the case, but I sometimes fear that social media makes it easy for people to go beyond the boundaries of debate and descend into personal abuse. It seems as if the facility to comment from the security or sometimes anonymity of a Twitter account has meant that the brakes on moderate language are off.

Finally, my experience tells me that politics and law-making only take you so far. Martin Luther King said, 'Laws may not change the heart, but they can restrain the heartless.' I believe that hearts can be changed, not by legislation, but by the power of the Gospel message. Arguably, 'Love your neighbour as yourself' is one of the most politically charged commandments in history.

Professor Frank Brennan SJ
Human rights lawyer and academic, University of Melbourne

There are almost 8 billion people now living on planet Earth. They live in 193 different nation states which make up the United Nations. Most human beings need to live in community with others. We are not able to live isolated on our own, providing for our own needs, and leaving everyone else to their own resources. Most of us are born into families where parents will have the primary responsibility for us in our early years. But not even parents can provide for all their children's needs, living isolated from their neighbours. It takes a village to raise a child. It takes a nation state to sustain all the villages in the area.

Neighbourhoods and communities are places and groups which are able to provide for their members. But not even the wealthiest and most powerful neighbourhood is able to provide for all the needs of its members. Just think about what needs to be done if someone in the community runs wild and threatens the safety and security of other members of the community. There is a need to call the police, or an ambulance or the fire brigade. Ultimately the services we all need can be provided only by the state.

Those who are in charge of the state have to be chosen or selected in some way. Those who exercise state power must be supervised and corrected when they go wrong. This means that you need a system of law and order. Our leaders need to be accountable, answering to the people for the laws and policies they propose.

Many laws and policies will be agreeable to most of the citizens. But some of those laws and policies will cause disagreement. Not everyone has to think the same about every issue in the state. That's where politics comes in. There are issues which require more debate. So, we need a means for allowing all points of view to be heard. In the end, a decision has to be made. Those who make the decision need to take responsibility for it. If they get it wrong, people might hold them to account. All this takes time. It's called politics. People argue about things that matter to them, and not just about what flavour of ice-cream they prefer.

When people find themselves in the minority, they sometimes get angry because they think those in the majority are not really paying sufficient attention to their views and their special needs. These are the things that matter. That's why they feature so much in the news. Other matters are set in stone and unlikely to change or are things that just don't matter. When you are left wondering why someone in politics gets angry, just ask yourself how you would feel if your parents were to impose their will on you without any discussion, insisting that you do something which you thought was wrong or not helpful for you. Wouldn't you get angry? Wouldn't you want them to give you a place at the table so you could be heard and understood. Securing that place at the table is politics.

29.

'Why do countries create conflict and war when the power of the leaders disappears when they die?'

THE PHILOSOPHER'S REPLY:

There are two elements to this question. The first relates to the reasons for war and the second the motivation of leaders. Let's deal with the second one first. Politicians seek power. Even if they are motivated by a wish to do good, without being in power they can achieve little. Once they achieve power, they wish to retain power and, later, often become concerned with how they will be judged by history. Although many are intelligent, most do not realise that despite their achievements and however great their reputation, they will eventually die and largely be forgotten so you are right to recognise this. The British Conservative party politician Enoch Powell said, 'All political lives, unless they are cut off in midstream at a happy juncture, end in failure, because that is the nature of politics and of human affairs.' The British Prime Minister, David Cameron, also quoted this when he resigned.

In terms of the first part of your questions. Nationalism and the feeling that 'my country is right' is a great contributor

WHY DO COUNTRIES CREATE CONFLICT AND WAR?

to conflict and people are rarely willing to listen to the views of an opposing country or to consider that the country they belong to may be in the wrong. War can be the final way of enforcing this view of the superiority of one's own country's interests – it has been described as 'the last refuge of the incompetent'. National pride may be, at least partly, a great evil as it tends to undermine the humanity of those who belong to a different tribe or country. Young men have in the past willingly and cheerfully gone off to fight without thinking through what they are doing or why – again nationalism plays a part in this.

There are many reasons behind war. There may be legitimate grounds – Britain entered the Second World War with great regret. The country did not want to fight as millions of men had been lost in the First World War. There was, nevertheless, a recognition that Hitler's Nazi regime represented a monumental tyranny that had to be stopped. If the war had not been fought then the lives of many, many millions more would have been lost. The United States refused to enter the Second World War until they were attacked by the Japanese at Pearl Harbour – they did not enter the war on principle. Hitler, by contrast, was motivated by a desire to restore the greatness of the German nation after the humiliation of the First World War and a conviction that Germany had a historic destiny to be masters of Europe. President Putin and Russia (supported incidentally by the Russian Orthodox Church) also wished to re-establish the glory days of the Russian empire and the people of Ukraine very bravely resisted this. It would be hard to argue that they were wrong to do so.

The United Nations has done an enormous amount to reduce conflict or to try to prevent an existing conflict spreading further. The effectiveness of the UN, however, depends on the co-operation of the great powers and often they do not agree and then nothing can be done. There are five permanent members of the UN Security Council and if any one of these votes 'no', then this represents a veto, and the UN can do nothing. Great powers also sometimes manipulate smaller countries to fight and to engage in what are called 'proxy wars' – so a powerful country may back one side in a dispute and another powerful country may back the other side – the two smaller countries fight without realising that they are being manipulated in what is in fact a 'great game' of international politics.

As people become better educated it is vital they become better informed. This is difficult as governments want their own population to see the world through their own eyes – the teaching of history in schools can contribute to this. Many countries teach history in a way that presents historical events in a way that is favourable to them rather than teaching it truthfully. The search for truth is, perhaps, the most important factor in stopping futile wars – but truth is very difficult to arrive at and means a willingness to consider that one's own country may be in the wrong and the media sources we rely on may be biased and, at least partially, inaccurate.

CHARLOTTE VARDY
Teacher and author

On one level 'countries' don't originate conflict. Rather, leaders do, dragging their countries along. Why? Because they can.

Famously, George Mallory said that he climbed Mount Everest 'because it is there'; while this seems an odd answer, really it taps into what it means to be human. Leaders have the power to do what we all - or at least most of us - would do if we had the power, to do things just because we could. The alternative, to do things not because we can but because we should, suggests that we are deferring to a higher power, which few of us would choose to do if we didn't have to. In this way, leaders do what they can because they can to prove that they are leaders and, in this way, to ensure that they won't die.

Most of us - if not all of us - lack the ability to imagine our own deaths or to believe that the world would carry on without us or imagine it as if we had never been born. This failure of imagination explains the human obsession with a God who plans each of our lives, knows and cares what we do and ensures our eternal existence. It can partly explain the human drive to marry and raise, rather than just reproduce and have children, the human desire to educate, to 'make a mark' and leave a legacy.

Most of us - if not all of us - lack the ability to understand our own powerlessness. This partly explains our tendency to believe that we can make things happen by performing rituals like saluting a magpie or throwing salt over our shoulders, that what happens to us depends on what we 'deserve'. Like babies, for good evolutionary reasons, we tend to imagine ourselves at the centre of existence and everything else existing for us, so we tend to connect what we do with what happens next.

While we grow larger, few of us grow out of the babyish world-view. Like most of us, leaders can't imagine their own irrelevance, so they do what they can to prove that they are relevant, which often means imposing their will on the world – violently.

Leaders create conflict because conflict is the essence of life. If you are fighting something, or something is fighting you, then you must be alive in some sense. When a leader is fighting, they are living, immortal so long as the fight continues. We 'live to fight another day' or 'go on fighting'. We fight cancer and other illnesses ... when we don't fight that is shameful, we lack 'fight' or 'succumb', 'defeated' by ...

The dominant culture prizes conflict over acceptance, so we aspire to fight. Leaders become leaders because they embody our aspirations; leaders create and sustain conflict because they are leaders and they are leaders because they represent what many wish to be. As the old saying goes, we get the leaders that we deserve ... we choose or at least tolerate the leaders we would be if we had half a chance.

In this way, when we blame Russia or Putin for dragging us into war, we should stop and think how Putin came to lead Russia and why Russia came to value warmongers as leaders. Isn't it true that the British - and Boris Johnson and his coterie in particular - see Churchill as the model of leadership, when Churchill said, 'we will fight them on the beaches ... we will never surrender'? How are we different?

On another level, countries - and really human societies in

general – create conflict and push their leaders towards war. Until human beings aspire to do what we should, not just what we can, and until the human imagination expands and can cope with our own irrelevance, we will be led towards war by the leaders we deserve.

HOW DO I MAKE SENSE OF PERSONAL RELATIONSHIPS?

30.

'What is love? Pop singers sing about love but as most relationships fail is it just attraction for breeding purposes like the pheasants, cows and sheep where we live?'

THE PHILOSOPHER'S REPLY:

Love is an overused word. It is used in many pop songs, children sign 'love' when writing to relatives and profess love of their parents even when their parents are in advanced old age and scarcely recognise them (although they may still reasonably and truthfully claim to love them). Brides and grooms promise to love one another till their death (even though many marriages end in divorce). Love has become trivialised and increasingly stands for sexual attraction. Most boys will be happy to say they love the girl they want to sleep with even though they give little thought to what this means. It is, therefore, perfectly reasonable to assume that 'love' has little meaning and might be a word expressed by a bull about to mate with a willing cow (if the bull could speak). Perhaps, however, there is more to it than this.

Throughout history there have been tremendous examples of people sacrificing themselves to save others.

In some cases, these are examples of parents doing so in order save children or immediate relatives and, in this case, their actions could be explained in terms of biology as some animals will do the same to protect their young. Yet there are innumerable other examples of love that is self-sacrificial. For Christians, of course, the perfect example of this is Jesus dying on the cross. By any reasonable standard he had lived a blameless life and had done nothing wrong and he could even have attempted a better defence before the Roman governor who condemned him. Nevertheless, he went to his death willingly and Christians believe he did so in order to save his followers and to bring them to his heavenly kingdom when they died. It is really a quite extraordinary story – the largest religion on earth with over two billion adherents has at its centre a man condemned as a criminal and killed in the most obscene and horrifying manner. In many ways, this has been sanitised with Christianity being turned into a matter of Easter Eggs and Father Christmas jumpers. In reality, however, it is about self-sacrificial love.

In J. K. Rowling's Harry Potter books, Dobby sacrifices himself to save his friend, Harry, and Harry's friends. When I run conferences with hundreds of teenagers in attendance the person that they most admire in the books is most often Dobby. Real love involves sacrifice. If anyone says to you 'I love you' it is worth asking them what precisely they mean by this. In should mean a willingness to put yourself in second place to the person you claim to love – to love them more (or at the very minimum equally) to the way you love yourself. This means loving them when they are in hospital, when their character changes, when they are impotent, when they suffer from depression, when they are old or suffering from Alzheimer's or other degenerative diseases.

Real love does exist and it is the most wonderful thing in

the world – but in human terms it is worth waiting a long time, if necessary, before you find it. The real question should not be 'Does he/she love me like this' but 'Do I really understand what it means for me to love like this?'. Much, much more uncomfortable still for a Christian the question should be 'Do I really love everyone I meet like this?'. Very few of us can answer 'yes' to either of the last two questions.

Professor Michael Barnes SJ

Professor of Interreligious Relations at the University of Roehampton

The statement that 'most relationships fail' is debatable. Whether or not it is true, it is a matter for empirical observation and strictly irrelevant to the question about whether there is more to love than 'attraction for breeding purposes'. Let's start with what it means to be human and the Aristotelian definition of human beings as rational animals. That does not mean we can be exhaustively defined in terms of a sort of dualism of physical and mental dimensions. While it may be plausible to grant a certain privilege to the claims of reason in considering what distinguishes humans from other animals, care needs to be taken not to collude with a reductionist account of human experience. What, for instance, of our capacity to respond as social animals capable of reflecting on and learning from encounters and meetings of all kinds that life-in-society involves?

Cognitive capacities *[human abilities based on the ability to use reason]* need to be related to or included within the less easily defined but equally important affective and emotional dimensions of human nature. Human consciousness of the way things hold together is formed by any number of factors, historical, cultural, psychological as well as the 'purely' biological. We exist, in short, as embodied persons. So, on the one hand, it would be fair to say that human beings are like pheasants, cows and sheep in so far as all animals enjoy sexual relations in order to sustain the species. On the other hand, human nature is a lot richer and more interesting than a superficial focus on the survival of the species suggests.

For Aristotle the purpose of human nature is about achieving *eudaimonia,* literally 'well-spirit' and usually translated as happiness or well-being. Love is a curiously diffuse concept and it is no surprise philosophers have taken very different approaches, from romantic obsession to empathetic altruism. But the task of the philosopher is not to come up with neat distinctions but to enable analysis to make better connections. It would be a curiously reductive *non sequitur* to say there is nothing significantly human in experiences of desire, friendship or attachment that provoke persons to find value and meaning beyond their own sense of self.

Pop singers – or indeed opera singers, for that matter – do not sing about love because they are obsessed with sex. Music, like culture and art of all kinds, is concerned to celebrate the most profound joys and sorrows of human loving – not just when we are taken out of ourselves in moments of great intimacy but when we feel the tragedy of loss, loneliness and separation. All the great religions know of the different manifestations of love – such as Christian *agape* or self-sacrificing service, Hindu *bhakti* or loyalty, Buddhist *karuna* or compassion. It is paradoxical, to say the least, that what makes us most deeply human is something that takes us out of ourselves and our ordinary mundane concerns – and raises questions about Ultimate Reality, Beauty and Truth.

PROFESSOR ROBIN DUNBAR

Anthropologist and Evolutionary Psychologist, University of Oxford

Love is rather a complicated word because we use it to mean several different things. 'I love carrots' doesn't mean the same thing as 'I love the way you laugh', never mind 'I love you'. The common thread here, perhaps, is something closer to the word 'like' meaning 'it gives me pleasure'.

The psychologist Robert Sternberg suggested that romantic relationships involve three separate dimensions: intimacy, commitment and passion. He called this his *Triangular Theory of Love*. Intimacy reflects feelings of emotional closeness and connectedness to a particular person, while commitment reflects a desire to be in their physical presence and do things for them. We might think of these as 'feeling close' and 'being close'. Passion, on the other hand, involves those feelings we associate with 'falling in love' : a sense of complete focus on the person in question, associated with feelings of exhilaration, with or without a sexual component.

The strength of a relationship – and its quality – is a consequence of how a relationship scores on these three dimensions. High scores on all three are reserved for romantic relationships, whereas high scores on just intimacy and commitment might characterise our relationships with parents, our 'best friend forever' and maybe even (some of!) our brothers and sisters. High scores on just intimacy or commitment (but not both) probably define more everyday friendships.

The important thing to appreciate is that this describes *how* we form relationships, not *why* we form them. These are two very different things. We form most of our relationships so as to provide ourselves with a variety of important benefits. These can range from someone to have fun with (party friends, if you like), someone to provide us with social or emotional advice and support (shoulders to cry on friends), or someone to create a family life with (a romantic partner). We typically have ten or twelve of the first kind, two or three of the second and only one of the last (at least at any one time).

Whatever benefits friends provide, we still need some psychological mechanism for creating the sense of friendship, otherwise nothing much would happen. You wouldn't give up your day to be with a stranger just so they would make you laugh or buy you lunch. What you need is some inner motivation to make you want to do that – which is where the Triangular Theory of Love comes in. And that also, perhaps, explains why relationships don't always last for ever.

The problem is that, just as it takes two to tango as the saying goes, so it takes two to make a friendship. For an intimate relationship to work and last, both of you must want to be friends with each other. If the two of you aren't completely in balance on the Love Triangle, one of you is always going to be less interested in sticking with the other, and the relationship will eventually fail. And that, of course, can happen over time as two friends, or even romantic partners, gradually change in their interests. There is no such thing as eternity in real life.

31.

'What is the point of an expensive wedding when so many marriages fail?'

THE PHILOSOPHER'S REPLY:

Marriages should be hugely significant events. They represent the formalising of a commitment between a couple that is intended to be for life – 'for better, for worse, for richer, for poorer, in sickness and in health, until death do us part'. Sadly, however, many people today do not see marriage in these terms. 'Pre-nuptial contracts' (these are formal contract drawn up before a marriage to decide how assets should be shared if the couple divorce) are increasingly common particularly if one party to the marriage is significantly wealthier than the other. Also, even as people get married, they cannot but be aware of the divorce rate. Despite this, marriages are significant. It is significant that the couple make formal promises to each other (and, if they are Christians, before God) and that these promises are made before witnesses. In the Catholic Christian tradition marriage is a sacrament and divorce and re-marriage is impossible. Most other Christian Churches do allow re-marriage, however. On marriage, the legal status of the couple changes and this is not the least part of the significance of the event – a couple who are living together have made no such commitment and the financial consequences of this in the event of the couple splitting up are huge.

Preparations for the 'big day' take time and this is good as it gives both parties a period in which to reflect on whether this is what they really want. When a couple marry and make their promises with their families gathered round, this reinforces the significance and importance of the event and can help relatives on both sides to assist the couple in making the marriage a success. Marriages require work and the initial emotional love tends not to last and should be replaced by a deep and developing friendship that should be maintained and grow with the passage of the years. This should, at best, endure and bind the couple together for life. Sadly, this often does not happen and that is because many relationships are transactional. What is a transactional relationship? It is one where the commitment of both parties is conditional on the behaviour of the other. 'You love me, and I will love you.' ' You support me emotionally, and I will support you.' 'You give me sexual satisfaction, and I will do the same for you.' 'You seek to make me happy, and I will seek to make you happy.' These relationships are common – why, after all, stay with someone who no longer meets your needs; who no longer loves you, who no longer supports you or gives you sexual satisfaction? These are perfectly reasonable questions, but they indicate the transactional nature of most marriage relationships.

The ideal of marriage is the one to which most couples aspire – an unconditional commitment which will deepen with the passage of the years. However, this requires patience, forgiveness, fortitude and work to make the marriage succeed and sadly, alas, many couples do not think in these terms.

FATHER CHRIS GLEESON SJ

Staff Chaplain at Xavier College and former Head of Riverview College, Sydney

Not all weddings are expensive, of course, and not all marriages

176

fail. Having been a Celebrant for several hundred weddings over many years, I believe that these ceremonies are important events for all those attending and participating. In the frenetic hustle and bustle of everyday life, a wedding congregation or audience is given an excellent opportunity to stop and reflect on some of life's non-negotiables. Weddings are a strong reminder to all of us of what is important in life – as Shakespeare wrote in one of his Sonnets:

> Love is not love
> Which alters when it alteration finds,
> Or bends with the remover to remove:
> O no! it is an ever-fixed mark
> That looks on tempests and is never shaken;
> It is the star to every wandering bark.

In his book, *Forgotten Among the Lilies*, Ronald Rolheiser OMI reflects on the sadness of men and women coming to him with the admission: 'It is so much easier to find a lover than a friend.' Irish singer, Mary O'Hara, makes the same point in *Celebration of Love*: 'Friendship or the capacity for it is a gift. I often think that relationships break up, not for lack of love, but for lack of friendship. In a society that is obsessed with the instant … friendships and personal loyalties which need time to mature … quickly become casualties.'

When we think about it, all of life is a journey into friendship –with oneself, with others, with our planet in need of healing, and most especially with God. It is very important to learn to be a good friend to ourselves. Irish writer John O'Donohue encapsulates this beautifully in his book *Anam Cara*, 'Soul Friend': 'You can never love another person unless you are equally involved in the beautiful, but difficult spiritual work of learning to love yourself.' Putting this another way, we need to maintain a fine balance in our souls between being both generous givers and receivers of friendship. In short, it is necessary for us to be generous to ourselves if we are to receive the love that surrounds us. Those people who love us release the best in us. As Joan Chittister says so well: 'They show us the face of our creating, caring God on earth.'

Many couples preparing for marriage choose among their service readings the famous chapter 13 of St Paul's first letter to the Corinthians which focuses on love and its practical manifestations. In 2018 I read a most interesting book titled provocatively, *The Attachment* – a book of correspondence between a senior priest friend of mine, Tony Doherty, and a younger woman playwright, Ailsa Piper. In talking about friendship, Ailsa wrote: 'Loving well is a life's work, isn't it.' How true that is, and that is what St Paul is saying to us in his Letter to the testy Church of Corinth. If I can put on my English teacher's hat for a moment, love is a verb, not a noun. Love is a doing word.

'Love is patient and kind; love never gives up; love is not jealous, conceited, or proud.'

Without love I am nothing, even if I have all the gifts and talents in the world. If I have not love, I am an empty shell. If you wish to put it into sporting metaphor, love is a marathon of the heart, not an emotional sprint. Like every marathon, love requires a good deal of hard work, disciplined training, and much endurance. Love is really tested in the hard yards. There was a senior priest of my acquaintance in Melbourne who used to say to young couples coming to him for marriage preparation: 'This marriage won't work, you know.' After they picked themselves up and got over their surprise, he would add: 'No. This marriage must be made to work.' Love is a choice we need to make every day – to be patient, kind, merciful and forgiving.

One of my favourite writers is a man named Jonathan Sacks, formerly the Chief Rabbi of the Commonwealth. When launching National Marriage Week some years ago in England, a pushy interviewer said to him: 'Isn't that very politically incorrect? Who really believes in marriage anymore?' To which the good Rabbi responded: 'I do, because in this buy it, use it and throw it away society of ours is there anything more lasting or more gracious than the commitment to share your life with the person you love, and, through that commitment, to bring new life into the world?' He went on to say:

'Marriage, sanctified by the bond of fidelity, is the nearest life gets to a work of art. It's what I call the poetry of the everyday. And though the moral fashions of today, like yesterday's papers, will one day crumble into dust, of this I am sure: marriage will still be there as the greatest remedy to our loneliness, the point where soul meets soul and we know we are not alone.'

MARRIAGE, SANCTIFIED BY THE BOND OF FIDELITY, IS THE NEAREST LIFE GETS TO A WORK OF ART.

32.

‘What is the point of
a funeral service?
They cost a lot.’

THE PHILOSOPHER'S REPLY:

I must admit to some personal bias when answering this question as I am not going to have a funeral service and did not attend the funeral services of my father or my mother. This may sound callous but there are good reasons for this. You are quite right that funeral services are expensive. When someone whom one loves dies, it is obviously a distressing time and many people will be emotionally vulnerable. They will miss the good times they shared with the person who died and, although they can do nothing about the fact that they have died, nevertheless they wish they could do something. They are therefore easily persuaded to spend more on a funeral than is strictly necessary. Many (not all of course) of those invited to a funeral feel that they ought to attend and do so out of duty.

The funeral address is sometimes given by a person who did not know the dead person at all. The focus in these addresses is normally about how wonderful the person who died was and how much she or he will be missed. Very rarely is the address in any sense balanced giving a picture of the person's weaknesses as well as any strengths. When the funeral is conducted by a priest, it may quite often happen that the person who died was not in any sense a religious believer, yet it is often assumed that she or he was – there is talk about the resurrection of the body when the dead person did not believe in this at all. Naturally this may be comforting for the relatives who are mourning but I am not sure it makes a great deal of sense.

Some people may find a funeral service psychologically helpful in coming to terms with their grief, and I can understand that this may be important. Having people gather round when someone has died is a primitive (in other words deeply basic) human reaction. Elephants sometimes do the same when one of their number dies. The funeral is a chance to catch up with distant members of the family that one may rarely if ever see except at occasions such as this.

When we die one of two things happens. Either the body rots or is burnt and that is the end of it. Humans are simply animals and life is at an end. The alternative is that there is a life after death. Christianity and Islam clearly proclaim the second of these. Socrates, preparing for his death as his friends mourned, asked why they were upset. Either, he said, death is a dreamless sleep (and there is nothing to be frighted of in this) or it is the most incredible adventure. I agree with Socrates, and I cannot see that having a funeral would make any difference at all to the outcome. Better, surely, to spend the money that would go on a funeral on donating to charity or any other purpose.

I appreciate that this may seem harsh, and I can only say that I can see no need or purpose for a funeral – unless some psychological need has to be addressed. In this case, a very simple funeral would be the most that might be appropriate. Millions of people die in wars, and no one may know where they are buried and certainly there would be no funeral service but, surely, this cannot make any difference to whatever (if anything) happens after death?

There is one further point. In the Catholic Christian tradition in particular prayers for someone who has died are held to be effective in reducing the amount of time she or he spends in purgatory (an intermediate state held by the Catholic Church to exist between death and the person of faith achieving the Beatific Vision of God). The Protestant reformers rejected the idea of purgatory – however even if it is valid, prayers can take place without a funeral service and, indeed, very often do.

THE REVD DR MARK OAKLEY
Dean and Fellow, St John's College, Cambridge

Not long ago, one of my heroes died. His name was Desmond Tutu and he had spent his life as a priest and bishop fighting racial injustice in South Africa, as well as many other evils around the world. He was awarded the Nobel Peace Prize and, when he died, the world mourned the loss of someone who had not only had such a strong moral compass within him, but also had lived courageously in upholding the dignity of each human being, whatever their gender, race, colour, sexual orientation or background happened to be. He was someone who refused to turn our diversity into division.

Everyone expected the great Archbishop Tutu to have a grand funeral. He had made clear, though, that he wanted the cheapest coffin with a few simple flowers on it, and, after his simple funeral service, he wanted his body to be aquamated because it is better for the environment than cremation. Seeing his small coffin lying in the cathedral reminded me of the day I saw a friend of mine in the army, who had been killed in Iraq, brought back in his coffin in an enormous transport plane on to the airport tarmac. His coffin was carried by his fellow soldiers and looked so small compared to the aircraft looming over it. And yet the flag draped over it, the waiting family, the officers and the chaplains, all gave that lonely coffin, like Desmond Tutu's in a quiet cathedral, a powerful dignity. They were all saying something by what they were doing - that his life mattered, his relationships mattered, and that what he, like all of us, uniquely brought to this world through his life, will always be of unnegotiable value.

You see, in this world all the things that matter most to us are somehow formed into a ritual. If we have a friend, we shake hands or hug. If we love someone, we kiss them. If we want to spend our life with someone, we make promises to them in front of our family and friends.

A funeral is similarly the way we begin to come to terms with the loss of someone who is part of our own life in some way. Even in death, we want to uphold their human dignity and to place their death for a short while in the context of reflections, memories and, maybe, prayers. It is a dramatic but sincere way of saying 'thank you' to them and for them. It is a ritualised way of saying 'goodbye'. If it is done in a religious setting, it is also a way of thanking God for them and commending them to God's safekeeping and peace. Their life is celebrated as a gift, created, mortal and beautiful, which is now placed back into the hands of their creator with gratitude for all they meant to us and for all they did.

Whether you are world famous or not known by many at all, whether you died in war or at home, whether expensive or cheap, a funeral is a vital way of acknowledging the death of someone unique and, afterwards, of seeing our own life as a gift to be lived to the full before we, too, finish our time on this complex and fragile earth.

HOW DO I MAKE SENSE OF RELIGIOUS BELIEFS?

33.

"The dinosaurs existed long before humans so how can the Bible be true as this does not fit with the Creation stories?"

THE PHILOSOPHER'S REPLY:

Since the nineteenth century it has become clear that the Hebrew and Christian scriptures that make up the Bible are complex documents of many different types compiled by different authors over the years. The Christian Gospels of Matthew and Luke contain the whole of Mark as well as material they have both drawn from a joint source which has been named 'Quelle' (for source) as well as their own material. Both the compilers of Matthew and Luke had their own agendas as they were writing for different audiences – Matthew primarily for Jews and Luke primarily for Gentiles.

There are two separate stories about creation in the first two chapters of the book of Genesis. Scholars consider they were written about 400 years apart. These are stories. They nevertheless both seek to show the dependence of the universe on God and that God is the origin of all that is: Also, that human disobedience and failure is a central part of human existence.

Too many Christians today, particularly in the United

States, do not recognise this complexity and take the Bible literally and this is no longer defensible intellectually. This does not necessarily mean that the Bible does not contain deep, profound and abiding truths. Truth can be conveyed in stories and, indeed, sometimes stories are more effective than conveying deep and abiding truths then any alternative. This is one reason why Shakespeare's plays have such enduring relevance – they are stories, however they provide profound truths about human affairs: about love, duty, conflict, jealousy, hatred, ambition, the relationship between men and women, politics and many other areas of life.

The answer to your question is simple. God may or may not exist. The universe may or may not depend on God. Life may or may not have meaning or purpose. The Bible claims that all these are true – atheists will say they are false. The issue, however, cannot be settled by the dating of dinosaurs.

THE RT REVD NICK BAINES
Lord Bishop of Leeds

I love dinosaurs. My children loved them and my grandchildren love them. I was sorry when the Natural History Museum in London swapped Dippy the Diplodocus for the skeleton of a huge blue whale.

There is no contradiction between the Bible and dinosaurs. The Bible is made up of many different types of writing: history, biography, narrative, philosophy, apocalyptic, poetry, and so on. The first chapters of Genesis fit into the 'poetry' category. Like any piece of writing, we also have to ask what question it is seeking to answer (or, at least, address). For example, if you read a crime thriller, you will find yourself unconsciously asking from the first page to the last: 'who dun it?' (especially if your grammar is bad). It is important to ask the right question of any text. The question Genesis is interested in is not 'How did everything come to be, and in what order?', but 'Why are things the way they are and what are we to understand and do about it?'. If you ask the wrong question, you won't find the right answer.

So, Genesis has no interest in the mechanics or stages of creation. It is poetry. When we read later in the Old Testament, for example, that 'the trees of the field clap their hands', we don't dismiss it on the grounds that trees don't have hands. We know what it means – truth goes deeper than facts.

Dinosaurs fit our world very well as life (pre-human beings) developed bit by bit. What is really interesting is that they seem to have been wiped out suddenly, possibly in a massive cosmic disaster. We still don't know how or why. But the fact that such animals could disappear so quickly ought to warn us (a) that all things are mortal, (b) even human beings don't have a right to live for ever, and (c) that we need humbly to pay attention both to the world itself and the implications of our own limitations. Love of God and a recognition of human failing is essential if we are to look and see and think and live humbly in this finite world.

I hope we will also continue to learn more about the dinosaurs and what a wonderful world it is that allows such creatures to have existed in the first place.

Canon THE Lady Ailsa Newby
Canon of Ripon Cathedral, England

There are, I think, two kinds of truth. The first kind of truth is a literal truth. It is sunny today. We can look outside and see if it's true. Queen Elizabeth II reigned in the UK for more than 70 years. That too, can be shown to be literally true by checking historical records. We can find this kind of literal truth in the Bible. Jerusalem exists as a city: we have evidence for this in history, and we can go and see it for ourselves. There is historical evidence that Jesus existed. So, to say Jesus existed is factually and literally true.

The second kind of truth is more a profound, underlying truth that seeks to explain why things are as they are in our world. So, although we know Jesus existed, the stories about how he was born have been written to explore a more profound truth that Christians believe about Jesus, namely that he was both fully human and also fully divine. They may not be literally true in the provable 'lets-look-out-the-window-and-see-if-it-is-true-that-the-sun-is-shining' sort of way but that is not the most important thing about them.

I like *The Lion, the Witch and the Wardrobe* as a story. It's fiction, but from it I'm helped to explore what Jesus may be like, through the story of what Aslan does to help the children and the people of Narnia. Stories like this are myths. They are not historically true, but they try to tell some truth about the profound truths of our world.

The Bible contains a lot of truth of this kind: imaginative stories that have been told to help us understand God. It does not matter that we cannot show they are literally true if they help us understand something about why we exist and how we might understand God. The ancient people who told the stories of how the world was created imagined how the world might have been created and how God might have been at the heart of that creation. If you read chapters 1 and 2 of the Book of Genesis you can see at once, anyway, that they cannot both be literally true because you cannot fit them together into one set of facts. Of course, the writers had no knowledge about dinosaurs or what science now tells us about the vast age of the universe and the place of our little planet Earth in it. They just knew about the natural world around them and they used what they knew to explore how human beings relate to God and the natural world.

Dinosaurs were part of God's good creation evolving through time. If the writers had known of them, I'm sure the stories would have been told differently. But it doesn't matter. The truth that Genesis teaches us is that, as humans, we are given the task of caring for God's world as it is.

34.

'How can God be a God of love when Jesus said many people would suffer terribly in hell? Would you make your children suffer like that if they did wrong?'

HOW CAN GOD BE A GOD OF LOVE WHEN JESUS SAID MANY PEOPLE WOULD SUFFER TERRIBLY IN HELL?

THE PHILOSOPHER'S REPLY:

Jesus was very clear about the existence of hell and that it was a place of exile from God and also a place of punishment. In the Middle Ages the terrors and pains of hell were emphasised by Christian preachers. Stained glass windows in Churches sometimes included the most graphic and terrifying pictures of people suffering for ever in hell. Jesus was sure that for those who went to hell there was no escape. Today, however, many Christians no longer think in these terms: instead they see hell as a place of permanent self-exile from God. The punishment is the recognition that, by their own choices, they have become permanently exiled from what human destiny is intended to be – namely dwelling in the presence of God.

Today Christians tend to emphasise that God is, above all, a God of love (Pope Francis constantly emphasises this theme) and if this is the case then the idea that anyone will for ever be tortured physically or psychologically seems hard to justify. It could be argued that if Jesus' teaching is to be treated as the ultimate authority, then he would not agree with what might be regarded as 'liberal' reinterpretation. Nevertheless, perhaps, hell has to exist as a concept as people have to be free to choose whether to live a life of goodness, kindness, forgiveness and love or instead to reject these values and to live for money, success, power and fame. The choices all of us make have consequences and the ideas of 'heaven' and 'hell' express these consequences whether either are literally true or not.

PROFESSOR C. STEPHEN EVANS
Baylor University, Waco, USA

This is a difficult question, and my own answer depends on my views of what hell is and why God allows hell. The Christian Scriptures contain many images of hell as involving pain and even torture. I believe these images are images and should not be taken literally. They are true in the sense that they convey how awful and fearful hell is, and how concerned we should be about avoiding that fate.

So what is hell, and why it is fearful? Almost all Christian theologians have affirmed that what is really awful about hell is that it means we are separated from God. To be in hell is to be apart from God, to have no connection with him. This is horrible because our deepest happiness is found in knowing God and becoming the selves God created us to be. Why does God allow humans to be separated from him? The answer is that he wants us to become his friends and serve him freely. However, he cannot give us the gift of freedom and then compel us to choose to serve him. (See my answer to Question 54.)

I believe God created hell out of love. This may sound strange, but here is why it is true. Heaven is wonderful not because it has streets of gold, but because in heaven we will be united in love with God and with all those who love God. Since God is the Good and God is Love, people who hate the good and choose hate over love would find God's presence unbearable. So God allows such people to separate themselves from him. The last merciful thing God can do for such people is to be free from having to endure his presence.

I personally believe that God does everything possible, even after death, to persuade people to love the Good. I believe, as C. S. Lewis did (see his book *The Great Divorce*), that the doors of hell are locked only from the inside. Anyone who really desires the Good and wants to live in Love will ultimately find God. The scary thing is that it may be possible for us humans to fix our character through repeated evil choices in such a way that God can do nothing to make us want to be his friends. That is what we risk when we do evil and spurn God's gracious offer to forgive our sins. People who do not want to be God's friends are in a way already in hell, even if they do not realize this and in some sense are getting what they want.

How many people wind up in hell? I think we do not know, and that Jesus is not really pronouncing on such matters. Rather, when he tell us that few people find the true way, he wants us to understand that we ought to seek God even if the way is lonely and few others join us, which will often be the case in this life. I think it is sound to hope that eventually hell will be empty, and God will persuade everyone to join his kingdom, but it is not reasonable to believe this, given what we observe of human behaviour.

35.

'The three Magi gave
baby Jesus gifts of Gold,
Frankincense and Myrrh
but we are told these point
to things that had not yet
happened such as Jesus' death,
so surely the stories can't
be true as they would
not have known what
was going to happen.'

THE PHILOSOPHER'S REPLY:

This question goes to the heart of how the Bible is to be understood. It cannot all be read as literally true – that is no longer possible. The creation stories in Genesis simply cannot be fitted in with modern understandings of the origin of the universe. The point you make about the three Kings is a perfectly valid one. The Three Kings (more accurately described as 'wise men') may or may not have existed, they may or may not have brought gifts, the gifts may or may not be accurately described. There was, after all, no one to record the story except for Mary and Joseph. The point about the story and about the story of the shepherds coming down from the hills and the angels is to show that, for Christians, Jesus is not just another human baby – his unique status is represented both by wise people, by the local ruler (Herod) and by people with little or no education (the shepherds were regarded as the lowest of the low in Jewish society as they could not keep to every letter of the law because of their jobs).

Jesus' birth is, for Christians, the hinge on which the universe turns. It is a decisive event in which God intervenes in human existence (this is called the Incarnation in which God become human and this is, or should be, what is celebrated at Christmas). Stories can convey deep truths: To dismiss the Bible which strongly influences the lives of more than two billion Christians across the world because it is not a literally true account is based on a radical misunderstanding. Much of Jesus' teachings were in stories or parables – no one thinks of these as literally true but they convey profound meaning.

The gifts brought by the three wise men all had meanings (as your question rightly indicates):

- Gold – this is intended to point to Jesus's kingship as gold was always associated with kingship.
- Frankincense – this points to Jesus' sacrificing himself on the cross for the sins of the world. Frankincense is a beautiful perfume that has traditionally been associated with sacrifice.
- Myrrh – this points forward to Jesus' death as this perfume, though less valuable than frankincense was used on the bodies of people who were buried.

If Christianity is true, then the Gospels are not recording a whole list of factual truths but rather truth at a much deeper and more profound level. It is a truth about God as a god of love who loves every human being no matter what they have done; who is always ready to forgive; who shows that human life is not about power, money, fame, reputation, and possessions, but about caring for each other, showing compassion, love and mercy wherever need is to be found. By reading the story of the Incarnation in this light it can be seen as seeking to convey a deep and profound truth.

FaTHer Dr RICHarD LeonarD SJ, PH.D.
Parish priest, North Sydney, Australia

When I began studying for the priesthood, we were told that at some stage in our formation we would have to spend a year addressing our personal issues professionally with a psychiatrist so that, potentially, we would not lump them on to others in the future. Of all the wonderful observations this psychiatrist made to me that year, among one of his best was, 'I know when someone has moved from adolescence to adulthood because they are not emotionally all or nothing.'

As an example, he gave me that of a 15-year-old girl who asks her parents for permission to go to a local dance. 'We would be delighted for that, darling,' says Dad, 'but Mom and I want you home by 10:30pm.' With a big pout, his adolescent daughter replies, 'Well I'm not going then. If I can't stay out until midnight like everyone else, then I won't go.' She doesn't go. For most adolescents, life is reduced to all or nothing, black or white, it's true or false. I know a good many 50-year-olds who are only 15 years of age emotionally.

This advice is helpful in approaching the Bible. Many young and not so young adults, believers and unbelievers alike, want the Bible to be either all true or all false. This position is theologically adolescent. The Bible is, literally, a library of books of varying relevance, importance, and application. Any one part of a particular book, and any one book within the Bible, needs to be read against the wider message of the Bible as a whole. This is especially true for Christians as we read parts of the Old Testament.

Though many of us were taught otherwise, by well-meaning preachers and teachers, for the last fifty years the Catholic Church has taught that the Bible is not to be interpreted literally. The Bible is not just all right or all wrong. Bernard Lonergan SJ, has offered a very helpful contribution in this debate. Lonergan makes a distinction between truth and fact. Although there are facts in the Bible, it was not written, and nor should it be interpreted as, a book of facts. It was written as stories, historical accounts, wisdom, poetry, prophecies, letters, parables and apocalyptic literature to evoke images, emotions, and responses to the religious truths it is setting out.

I can see why Richard Dawkins could say, 'The God of the Old Testament is arguably the most unpleasant character in all fiction: jealous and proud of it; a petty, unjust, unforgiving control-freak; a vindictive, bloodthirsty ethnic cleanser; a misogynistic *[a hatred of women]*, homophobic *[a hater of gay people]*, racist, infanticidal, genocidal *[killing people because of their race]*, filicidal *[killing his own son]*, pestilential *[sending plagues]*, megalomaniacal *[concerned only with power]*, sadomasochistic *[interested in pain and suffering]*, capriciously malevolent bully.' Conveniently, what Dawkins does not say in his selective caricature is that there are many more instances in the Old Testament where God is also presented as loving, forgiving, gentle, compassionate, just, merciful, faithful, and joyous.

When it comes to Jesus, however, there is not a single moment in the New Testament when Jesus is petty, unjust, an unforgiving control-freak, vindictive, a bloodthirsty ethnic cleanser; a misogynist, homophobic, racist, infanticidal, genocidal, filicidal, pestilential, megalomaniacal, sadomasochistic or a capriciously malevolent bully.

The story of the three Kings, therefore, should not be seen as a factual account but rather as expressing something profound about the nature of Jesus and his life – which is why the gifts the Kings are meant to have presented are described as they are.

36.

❝Jesus said that no one should call anyone good except for God and this seems to mean that Jesus was not the same as God? Did Jesus believe in the Trinity?❞

THE PHILOSOPHER'S REPLY:

The Christian doctrine of the Trinity – that the one God is made up of three separate persons (Father, Son and Holy Spirit) is at the heart of Christianity. This idea separates Christians from Muslims and Jews as although all three religions firmly maintain that God is one, Christians maintain that God is both one and three at the same time. This was important as Christians developed the idea that Jesus was God in God's self, become incarnate (in other words being born as a human baby). This seems, however, to mean that Jesus came into existence at his birth and Christians wished to deny this maintaining that it was God in God's self who became human and Jesus (the second person of the Trinity) was part of the Trinity from the creation of the universe.

It seems unlikely that Jesus himself would have known of the doctrine of the Trinity and the example you give of Jesus saying that only God should be called good is an example of this. In yet another passage Jesus says very clearly, 'my father is greater than I' (Jn 14:28), which is precisely what the idea of the Trinity rejects. However, when Jesus' disciples asked Him to show them God he said 'whoever has seen me has seen the Father' – thus implying the doctrine of the Trinity. Whether Jesus himself actually said this it is impossible to know. It is, perhaps, significant that this reference occurs in the Gospel of John (14.9) which scholars consider was written much later than the other Gospels (possibly around 130CE although the dating is disputed), and this makes it more likely that whoever compiled the Gospel of John might have inserted this as if the scribe believed in the Trinity it might have been the sort of thing that Jesus would say.

The early Church would have claimed three things:

1. That Jesus was baptised by John in the River Jordan.
2. That Jesus told his followers to go out into the world and tell everyone about Him and baptise them in his name.
3. That after Jesus rose from the dead, he promised that the Holy Spirit would be sent to his followers.

Given these three positions, it might have seemed obvious to anyone writing about Jesus that he would have commanded his followers to baptise in his name and, assuming Jesus was God, that anyone seeing Jesus would also be seeing God.

RT REVD PETER CARNLEY AC
Former Primate of the Anglican Church of Australia

When Jesus asked this question, he was not necessarily being coy, or denying his unique sense of identity, but rather prompting a question: 'If you are discerning something in me that prompts you to call me 'good', then perhaps you at least need to take me seriously as the agent of the revelation of God, for there is really none perfectly good but God.'

Even so, Jesus cannot have believed in the doctrine of the Trinity. This basic Christian doctrine was only really formulated by a group of theological thinkers in Cappadocia (now a region of southern Turkey) during the course of the fourth century AD. These very gifted thinkers are usually called the 'Cappadocian Fathers' – Basil of Caesarea, his brother Gregory of Nyssa, and another Gregory from Nazianzus. Given that Jesus lived some centuries before this, he cannot have believed exactly what they formulated concerning the Trinity. After all, the human Jesus was a man of his time; he did not know of the existence of Australia or that Donald Trump would be a hopeless President of the USA either.

Nevertheless, there is a very strong tradition that Jesus himself referred to God as his 'heavenly Father', and his first disciples certainly appear to have seen him as 'God's Son' in some unique and special sense. We cannot be sure that Jesus himself said 'who has seen me has seen the Father', but certainly those words were attributed to him (by St John in his Gospel), and another early tradition spoke of Jesus as 'the express image of the invisible God' (the Epistles to the Colossians and Hebrews). Still others saw Jesus as uniquely anointed with the Spirit of God. Certainly, the early Christian believers came to the conviction that the Spirit of God was shown in his words and works as a uniquely impressive love.

Especially after the death of Jesus, the first believers came to perceive the presence of this very same loving Spirit, no longer just as something remembered, but as living still, informing and transforming their lives. St Paul, for example, declared that Jesus had become 'a life-giving Spirit' and went on to refer to it indiscriminately as 'the Spirit of Christ' and also as 'the Spirit of God' (e.g. in Romans 8).

The Cappadocian Fathers were faced with the task of making some systematic sense out of the rich and varied tradition of language of this kind to which the first Christian believers had turned in trying to communicate something of the impact that the remembered Jesus had made upon their lives and that they now knew in the Christian fellowship.

In their development of the doctrine of the Trinity the Cappadocian Fathers made explicit what had been discerned as implicit in the original encounter of the first disciples with Jesus:

- whether they spoke of God the Father, or
- of the revelation of God the Father in the historical life of Jesus, or
- their conviction of the animating Spirit that characterized the communion they themselves knew in the Christian fellowship, they had to do with substantially the very same inter-personal divine reality.

They were all speaking of the same Reality. Jesus may not have himself believed in the Trinity; but the encounter with him introduced the first believers to the mystery of an inter-personal spiritual reality that eventually led them to speak of One God and Three Persons, Father, Son, and Spirit.

37.

❝Jesus said not to worry about food, drink or clothing but some mothers cannot afford to feed their children and schools are having to provide breakfasts for hungry children. We have loads of food banks and old people have to choose between eating and heating. How can it be that they should not worry about these things as well as the environment even if they don't affect us?❞

THE PHILOSOPHER'S REPLY:

You are quite right – people must worry about these things. Similarly, if one is in a war zone or one of your relatives had been locked up by repressive regimes for expressing opinions that go against the government of the day or a child is desperately ill, then worry and concern is inevitable.

It is human and it is right. The only way I can explain what Jesus said is that there is a difference between the perfectly reasonable and right concerns that you list and a more radical worry and doubt about how things will turn out in the future. Jesus recognised there would be wars and many troubles and at times everything would seem pointless and hopeless. Despair would be very easy and appealing. Yet at the end of the day, faith means believing that good will triumph over evil and hope will triumph over despair. In addition, of course, if one is a Christian life will triumph over death. Death does not have the last word, nor does illness, nor does poverty. However hopeless things may seem at the time, ultimately all shall be well. I fully recognise and accept that if one is in extreme suffering then this seems unreasonable and, indeed, impossible – but that is where faith comes in.

When the Prophet Elijah was in the desert, everything seemed hopeless. The Queen, Jezebel, had imported her own gods, all the priests of Yahweh, the God of the Jews, had been put to death and Elijah saw himself totally alone and Jezebel was having him hunted down to put him to death. By any rational standards there were good grounds for ultimate despair – yet this was to prove mistaken. Jezebel died, the statues of her gods were destroyed and so were their priests and the worship of Yahweh was reinstated. The survival of the Jews and their faith is one of the most extraordinary and almost unbelievable historical facts. They have been persecuted by many civilisations, Christianity tried to wipe them out, they have been ostracised and oppressed. Almost all other ancient religions and sects have disappeared - but Judaism has remained.

Concern, therefore, about all those things you list is absolutely understandable and right but, nevertheless, Christians retain hope and the conviction that, at the end of the day 'All shall be well and all manner of things shall be well' as Julian of Norwich said. Julian of Norwich was one of England's most significant mystics. She lived through the Black Death – one of the most appalling plagues ever to have struck Europe with an enormous death toll. She wrote the earliest surviving book in the English language to be written by a woman, *Revelations of Divine Love*. Her message of hope, in spite of all the apparently overwhelming evidence to the contrary, is still held by Christian today.

Professor Tom McLeish FRS

Professor of Natural Philosophy in the Department of Physics, University of York

It's important to note that, although the Bible was written in a way that is helpful to us, it was not written directly to us, but through people to other people in their own times and places. So we need to know what those people thought, what their ideas were and the stories they told and understood about the world, if we are to understand the Bible in a way helpful to us. In the Sermon on the Mount in Matthew's Gospel, chapter 6, that you refer to, Jesus was at the beginning of a radical ministry of prophecy, healing, and pointing out to the people of Roman-occupied Palestine that God was indeed going to fulfil ancient promises of rescue, and healing of the world through them, but not in the way that they had assumed. It would be necessary to follow him in a very different way, including leaving livelihoods (like the fishermen Peter and John) for this to happen. Jesus was telling them to focus on that healing mission - which he called the 'kingdom' - while that was happening, not on their daily routine as before.

So Jesus was not saying 'don't worry about the environment' to people 2000 years later. On the contrary - if you follow the long story of what that idea of 'kingdom' means, then one of the things it means is that the Earth is ours on trust to look after! So when using the Bible it is very important to read it in context' - of the people and events at the time, and as part of a long story of which we are a part.

Doing this, we do it honour and justice. To pull out a line out of context and assume we can interpret it as if it were someone like a schoolteacher talking to us this morning is not doing it justice at all.

38.

'Is it a coincidence that all major Christian events are on a Sunday or are they all made up?'

THE PHILOSOPHER'S REPLY:

The Hebrew scriptures say that the universe was created in six days and on the seventh day God rested. The creation stories are literally that – stories – but the idea of rest from labour is an important one and the Jews always insisted that on one day a week no work was to be done. Life should not be about perpetual work; there has to be time for families, friends and recreation and, if one believes in God, for God as well. Jews, Christians and Muslims recognised the importance of this and Sundays were kept aside as a day of rest in Christianity (in Islam it is a Friday and in Judaism a Saturday). Until quite recently, in Western countries, shops remained shut on Sundays and no one did any work except for the emergency services. It therefore made sense for some Christian events to be remembered on a Sunday. In a way the dates were originally arbitrary, but it is no less significant because of that.

Not all Christian events occur on Sundays. Jesus' birth, for instance, is commemorated at least in Western Christianity on 25 December and this falls on different days of the week depending on the calendar. Ascension Day (the day when the resurrected Jesus is held by Christians to have ascended to God) is on a Thursday. We do not know on what date Jesus was born and 25 December was chosen as it is close to mid-winter's day and traditional Pagan festivals were held on this day. The fact that 25 December was chosen by the early Church does not diminish the importance of remembering the incarnation. Christmas is commemorated as one of the most important dates in which Christians remember God becoming human in Jesus. In the case of Christian celebrations of Easter, this follows the dating of the Jewish Passover so the dates vary each year but Jesus' resurrection is always celebrated on a Sunday as this was two days after the Passover.

Judaism, Christianity and Islam share a wish to mark out one day a week as a day of special religious significance when ordinary work concerns take second place. Which day is chosen may in some cases be relatively arbitrary but the importance of the idea of one day of each week being dedicated to something other than work and shopping remains important.

39.

**'Would Jesus want expensive
cathedrals, bishops in robes,
etc. Would that be what he
would want?'**

THE PHILOSOPHER'S REPLY:

The short answer has to be 'no'. In many ways, according to
the Gospels, Jesus was a very simple person concerned with
the needs of those who were poor and vulnerable as well
as those who ignored what was really important in life and
instead focussed on money, power, fame and the like. There
is no evidence at all that he would have wanted the wealth,
power, ceremony and pageantry which has become such a
part of many (not all) Christian Churches.

Having said that, human beings are human and Christianity
has been responsible for some of the most sublime music,
architecture and painting. The beauty of Cathedrals and the
liturgy with all its pomp and ceremony have drawn many
people closer to a transcendent dimension on life (in other
words to an appreciation of what lies beyond the mundane,
material world) and brought millions to re-evaluate their lives
and to recognise that their previous priorities were mistaken
and likely to lead to disappointment. Much of the wealth
and power of the Churches arose in the Middle Ages when

Churches became incredibly rich and Bishops, Cardinals and others lived like the most wealthy Princes with vast estates, servants, castles and their own armies. Much of the pageantry originates from these times but this is no longer the case today.

In so far as music and architecture moves people to appreciate beauty and the transcendent then it has a value but in too many cases these have become ends in themselves. Frequently the primary function of many Churches and priests has become about maintaining historical buildings (often as tourist attractions) and their original purpose has become marginalised. In a sense, therefore, it could be argued that in this respect some Churches at least have lost their way.

FATHER DR RICHARD LEONARD SJ, PH.D.
Parish Priest, North Sydney, Australia

Pope Francis said: 'Every major study of belief and unbelief says that for many people it is not only a deity that is the major stumbling block to religious faith, but also the lives of religious individuals and collectives who claim to follow that God … It is a good challenge for us to practise what we preach and to follow Jesus' service, humility, and simplicity.' Pope Francis, therefore, would understand what lies behind your question.

It is true that Jesus was a poor man who preached a gospel about lifting up the poor, the marginalized and the oppressed, and who said that not only do we have an obligation to share but that we will be happiest when we are free of the possessions that keep us from loving God and our neighbour. He also knew that love of money was one of the greatest dangers to us losing our very selves. There is no question that for the first three hundred years of the Christian Church's life, it lived the simplicity Jesus lived. In fact, given that many people died for their Christian faith, their witness to a sacrificial life is above reproach.

It is easy to judge what later became the Roman Catholic Church and its subsequent claims to power and wealth as a betrayal of what Jesus proclaimed. It certainly was a betrayal, but it also provided social stability and cohesion in very desolate times. In 2012, *The Economist* estimated that the US Catholic Church was worth around $170 billion, of which $150 billion was estimated to be in the assets and real estate of US Catholic healthcare, welfare, and education institutions.

In his book, *Things You Get for Free*, Michael McGirr tells the story of going on pilgrimage to Rome with his mother. Maureen McGirr had always wanted to see St Peter's Basilica. Michael records the big day. 'I looked up into the dome that Michelangelo designed late in life: he never lived to see it finished. In that moment, hundreds of visitors rushed past. 'What on earth are they trying to prove?' I was distracted by the noise. 'When you think,' said Mum, leaving her sentence unfinished … 'When you think what?' I asked … 'I don't know. When you think.' 'What?' I was getting testy with her. Mum drew in breath to say something important. 'When you think that Jesus had nothing.' It was a naked response. For seventy years, this building had stood as the physical centre of Mum's religion. This was her pilgrimage to Mecca. Yet her response was almost revulsion.

On the other side of the ledger, it is good to remember that the wealth of the Church is not only and simply about power for its own sake. It also runs an enormous number of charities doing wonderful work across the world as well, of course, as financially assisting hundreds of its 2,946 dioceses to provide local services, on every level, for believer and unbeliever alike.

The real challenge is learning from the avarice and

triumphalism of some of the previous generations of the Church. Living simply with what we need rather than what we want, sharing everything with the poor, who are at the centre of the gospel, and being a voice for the voiceless in many circles in which the Church lives might be the even bigger and more exciting challenges. It is this that Pope Francis is calling Catholics throughout the world to achieve.

DAVID GARRATT

Writer and former Principal Daramalan College, Canberra ACT, Australia

A very good question. Jesus was much more concerned about the poor, the sick and the persecuted people than about grand buildings or fine clothes. His life, as we know it, was very simple and I feel sure he would rather more money be spent on helping the vulnerable people in our society than on fine monuments and robes. However, the impressive buildings serve a purpose for us as humans, providing a sense of wonder and inspiration, a place of quiet where prayer as a community is supported. The money being spent on the Sagrada Familia in Barcelona is creating such a building. I found my visit there quite uplifting. I can still recall the awe I felt in the beauty of the place. Jesus, I think, would be happy for people to be so enriched. At the same time, the primary concern for the poor must be kept in mind.

Costumes add to the effect of many celebrations in our lives and the Church 'costumes' are no different. While the fine robes have a place in the celebrations of the church rituals, they tend to be overdone. Simpler forms of dress might be found which still play a part in meaningful ceremonies.

40.

‘The Bible is a mixture of stories how are we meant to know which are true and which are made up stories to make a point?’

THE PHILOSOPHER'S REPLY:

It depends on what one means by 'true'! I know this seems a common answer given by philosophers but in this case it really does apply. If by 'true" is meant literally true, then there is no way of demonstrating that all the stories in the Bible are true and in some cases, it is clear that, taken literally, they are false. Stories can, nevertheless, show truth at a deeper level. The two creation stories in Genesis are certainly not literally true but probably they were not intended to be. They were stories made up long after the events to try to explain the belief that the universe was created by and depended on God, and that obedience to God was the road to human fulfillment. Understood like this the stories may indeed be true. The same applies to the stories of the Wise Men at Jesus' birth (c.f. Question 35) and to many other stories.

The Bible needs to be read as a whole rather than in small sections. The same applies in Islam to the Qur'an. Islamic scholars argue that it is necessary to see the text as a unity and not to pick out individual sections isolated from the rest of the text. Read as a unity, countless millions of people throughout history have found in it a profound source of wisdom and inspiration. In fact, no other single book has sold so many copies as has the Bible and no other single book has had so profound an influence. There are, naturally, differences as to how the tests will be interpreted. This does not mean, however, that there are not deep, abiding truths lying beneath the surface.

THE MOST REVD AND RT HON Stephen Cottrell
Archbishop of York

Think of the Bible as a library rather than a book. This helps in three ways. First, you don't need to start at the beginning. You wouldn't do that in a library! Secondly, there are different types of books, fiction and non-fiction; and the non-fiction has all sorts of categories from car mechanics to quantum physics. Thirdly, all the books - fact and fiction - are true, but we intuitively recognise that each contains a different type of truth.

Take, for example, Shakespeare's *Romeo and Juliet*. It's in the fiction section. Only very loosely based on fact, Shakespeare made it up. But would you say it isn't true? Of course not. It's what you might call poetic or philosophic truth. It perfectly portrays the truth of love and the horrors of division and prejudice. On the other hand, over in non-fiction, there are recipes, where the facts really do matter: one teaspoon of salt, not a whole bag! But also, history, where the truth of what happened long ago is written by someone alive today, whose account is shaped by their interpretation of the events as well as the records of what happened, some firsthand.

With this in mind, you can open the Bible with confidence. Written by the followers of God over many centuries, it's a collection of books, not one book with one author. There are different books with different truths, so you need to know where you are in the library. The opening chapters of the book of Genesis, for instance, are not factual, scientific accounts of how the world was made. We're in the poetry section. But it is a beautiful account of why. It also explores why things go wrong. Large parts of the Old Testament are history, telling of judges and kings, exile, and conquest, as the people of God, the Jews, learn how to serve one God with one purpose. There are also books of law, philosophy and poetry, all with different kinds of truth.

The centre of the Bible, for Christians, are the four gospels. Resting on first-hand accounts of Jesus, they are a reliable, historical record, but each is written with a particular slant for a particular purpose for a particular community of Christians. That's why they differ. This isn't a problem. It demonstrates how truth itself is multifaceted. Within the gospels are the stories Jesus told. He made them up. Like *Romeo and Juliet*, the parables of the Good Samaritan and the Prodigal Son contain deep and poignant truth. Then there are the letters Paul wrote. They are actually the earliest bits, written only about 30 years after Jesus' death.

So, all of it is true, which does not mean some of it isn't made up. And all of it is inspired by God so that in reading the Bible (though not necessarily from the start) we can learn about the heart of God and what it means to be human.

Professor Zohar Hadromi-Allouche

Professor in Classical Islamic Thought, Trinity College, Dublin

The short answer is, we cannot always tell, and it does not necessarily matter. As far as the Bible is concerned, we are meant to accept all these stories as true stories that make points. To some extent, if a story makes a good point, it doesn't really matter whether it reflects historical events or not. It might echo values, moral questions, or other challenges which humans face continuously — sibling rivalry (Cain and Abel, Rachel and Leah, Joseph and his brothers), barrenness (Sarah, Rachel), family sagas (house of Saul), and more. A story can help us better understand the situation we are facing in our own lives, see it in a new light (such as the story of the poor man's sheep, which made David realise the extent of his injustice towards Uriah), and even derive operative conclusions.

Moreover, as long as many people believe that a given story is true, and choose to behave in light of this belief, the story is as good as true in that it affects human behaviour in the 'real' world — regardless of its historicity. Some people, however, find that this last point makes it crucial to know which stories are true. By clarifying whether or not a story is 'true,' they hope to change human behaviour. For this purpose, several methods are being used. One of them is archaeology. For example, in the scholarly debate regarding whether or not King David was a historical figure, the former view has received a strong support in recent years, following the discovery of relevant archaeological sites and artifacts (e.g., an inscription mentioning the House of David). This finding has a contemporary significance since the historicity of David is used as an argument in the Israeli-Palestinian conflict. However, did these findings settle this conflict? Not yet.

Furthermore, archaeology cannot answer all our questions. It can confirm that David was a historical figure, yet it remains difficult to assess whether all biblical stories about him are historical. Here other methods of inquiry can be useful. For example, textual analysis of a given biblical story, or its comparison with other texts, with similar content, or emerging from the same era or geographical region. The story of David and Goliath (1 Sam 17), for example, has a parallel within the Bible itself (2 Sam 21:19), which tells about a person named Elhanan who killed Goliath. For some, this parallel indicates that David had an additional name, Elhanan, but it might also be that initially this story was unrelated to David, and only later it became linked with him, to glorify the King. Perhaps it never even happened. We will probably never know. But what we do know, is that we still enjoy and derive inspiration from a story about the underdog who got the upper hand by being resourceful, having firm belief, and refusing to be intimidated by a menacing rival. Therefore, an engaging, thought-provoking story can be of true value for us, even if it is not historically true.

41.

‘One of our teachers said the story of Job was about God having a bet with Satan and killing his family and animals and torturing him. If a human being did this he would be put in prison for life. How does this make any sense?’

THE PHILOSOPHER'S REPLY:

The story of Job is ultimately about the demand for the believer to have faith and trust in God in spite of all the evidence to the contrary.

Job suffers appallingly and his suffering is not justified. He had been a good man throughout his life, yet he loses everything. His so-called friends suggest that he is being punished but he cannot accept that – he does not deserve the suffering he is experiencing. Above all it is a story about the importance of hope. Hope in the face of circumstance that, rationally, should only point to abject despair. Any rational and reasonable person would curse God and hope to die as, indeed, Job wishes. It is also a story about holding on not just to hope but to trust when all the evidence seems against it.

I am a philosopher and, to philosophers, rationality reigns supreme. The story of Job maintains that philosophers are limited. Reason does not have all the answers. The brilliant mathematician Blaise Pascal put it well when he said, 'The heart has its reasons that reason cannot understand'. Millions of people down the centuries have held on to hope, trust and faith that - in spite of overwhelming rational evidence to the contrary - beauty, love and hope will triumph over despair. Rationally this cannot be defended and there is no adequate philosophical defence but, towards the end of a life devoted to studying philosophy, I am more and more convinced that reason does not have all the answers. It is interesting the great poets like William Blake came to the same conclusion as do modern writers such as Phillip Pullman who was and is strongly influenced by William Blake.

C. S. Lewis has a wonderful story of the Marsh-wiggle (don't ask me what this is!) called Puddleglum who is captured by a witch and imprisoned with some children in a magical underground kingdom. She seeks to convince them with the aid of magic that life is pointless, there is no such thing as beauty and love and they should recognise this. Yet the Marsh-wiggle holds on and, in so doing, he overcomes her power and finds release (with the children) from the witch's spell. I have to say I am on the side of the Marsh-wiggle.

There is another important element to the story of Job. It rejects the then commonly-held idea that prosperity and health are due to being favoured by God and sickness and poverty are due to God's displeasure with an individual. Job's so-called comforters, his friends, favoured this position and the book of Job shows that it is nonsense. This was an important insight and has contemporary relevance not least among supporters of what has become called 'prosperity theology' which holds that God grants wealth and success to those who worship God – and who give money to certain Churches. This is a travesty of everything Christianity or Jesus himself traditionally stood for.

Rabbi Professor Dan Cohn-Sherbok
University of Wales

I think your teacher did not explain the story accurately. The Book of Job is about the theological problem of human suffering. The book contains 42 chapters in the form of a series of dialogues between Job and his friends. In the prologue, Satan questions the sincerity of Job, known as a pious and virtuous man. He claims that Job is obedient to God only because of the favours he has received. To test Job's obedience, God permits Satan to bring upon Job all sorts of misfortunes. His wealth is taken away, then his beloved children die, and finally he is afflicted with a loathsome disease.

In the dramatic dialogue between Job and his three friends, the question of undeserved suffering is discussed. Job, shaken by numerous misfortunes and sufferings, pours out his soul in bitter protest against God's unjustifiable punishment and proclaims his innocence. His friends, however, insist that Job confess his guilt, because God's punishment, though not always understood by human beings, is nevertheless always deserved.

In the epilogue, describing God's appearance in a storm out of which He spoke to Job, Job is told to realise how insignificant human beings are in the face of God's omnipotence *[the idea that God is all powerful]*, and how futile is the attempt to understand his ways. First God asks Job about understanding of creation: 'Where were you when I laid the foundations of the earth? Tell me, if you have understanding. Who determined its measurements—surely you know! Or who stretched the line upon it? On what were its bases sunk, or who laid its cornerstone, when the morning stars sang together and all the sons of God shouted for joy?' (38:4-7).

Confessing his ignorance, Job accepts that he cannot fathom God's ways: 'I know that thou canst do all things, and that no purpose of thine can be thwarted. Who is this that hides counsel without knowledge? Therefore I have uttered what I did not understand, things too wonderful for me which I did not know' (42:1-3).

You may not find this answer satisfactory. Yet, it has provided comfort for Jews through the centuries in the face of suffering and death. Such an answer to the problem of human suffering does not seek to reconcile human misery with God's omnipotence. Instead, we are told that human beings simply cannot comprehend God's unfathomable ways. Instead of seeking to formulate a theological explanation for human misery, we should, like Job, accept God's mysterious providence [the outworking of God's purposes through history].

42.

'In Islam the prophet was allowed by God to have 12 wives and married one of them when she was 9 years old. He was meant to be the perfect human being so was this right?'

THE PHILOSOPHEr'S rePLY:

Islam has a problem with this question. The Qur'an is held to have been dictated to the Prophet Muhammed by the angel Gabriel and it is blasphemy in Islam to claim that the Prophet himself had any influence at all on the text: The Qur'an is the divinely dictated word of God. There are some passages in the text of the Qur'an which seem to indicate behaviour or commands which, by modern standards, would be considered unacceptable. Serious Islamic scholars deal with this issue by saying that it is important to regard the text of the Qur'an as a whole and not to pick out selected verses and treat them as independent of the rest. In many ways there are similarities with the life of the Prophet.

Muslims do, indeed, hold that the Prophet lived a perfect human life – yet, as you say, he married 12 wives (not all at the same time) and married his youngest wife when she was six although did not consummate the marriage with her until she had her first period (on some accounts about nine years old but on others a few years later). It is still the practice in some Islamic societies for girls to be able to marry and then to have sex soon after their first period. When the government in Pakistan tried to introduce a law prohibiting marriage under the age of 16, this was held to be 'UnIslamic' by the supreme Islamic religious authorities.

The best answer might be to say that having 12 wives is not the standard approved in Islam. A man may only have four wives at a time and then only subject to strict conditions including that they all be treated fairly and that he has the wealth to be able to maintain them all. The Prophet lived at a certain time and we know that some of his wives were previously wives of his followers who fell in battle so he could be argued to have been honourable in seeking their protection.

Whether it is 'right' to have four wives or for a girl to marry and have sex after puberty will largely depend both on whether one is a Muslim and secondly on the status given to the text of the Qur'an. As in so many cases when dealing with religious ethics, opinions differ. Non-Muslims would, however, be almost completely united in claiming that both are wrong.

Professor Zohar Hadromi-Allouche
Professor in Classical Islamic Thought, Trinity College, Dublin

From a religious perspective, all actions of the Prophet, who was the divinely-inspired messenger of God, were right. Indeed, charismatic leaders often do things that are forbidden to their followers. Moses, whom God entrusts with the tablets of the

JESUS, WHO PREACHED FOR LOVE
AND COMPASSION, CURSED AND
KILLED A FIG TREE FOR NOT BEARING
FRUIT OUT OF SEASON .

covenant gets away with killing a man (Exodus 2:12; 31:18). Jesus, who preached for love and compassion, cursed and killed a fig tree for not bearing fruit out of season (Mark 11:12–14). The implicit assumption is that a leader may do things that the followers may not. In the case of Muhammad, this means that despite being the perfect human being and a role model, not all his actions are to be followed by others. Particularly, his multiple marriages disagree with Qur'anic law, which limits the number of wives to whom a man may concurrently be married to no more than four.

A different argument that is often made in this context is the need to consider things within their historical context. Notably, all Muhammad's wives, save Aishah, were divorcees or widows. Hence it is assumed that the multiple marriages served to support and provide for these women. This might be contrasted with that of Muhammad's first wife, Khadijah, whom he married before he became an active prophet (before the Qur'an was revealed to him), was also a widow, yet she was rich, ran her own business, and was Muhammad's employer before their marriage. Their marriage was monogamous, and lasted for 15 years, until Khadijah died. However, whether or not Khadijah's character, and marriage with Muhammad, were normative of seventh-century Arabia remains to be determined.

Moreover, Muhammad's multiple marriages following Khadijah's death coincided with his gradual emergence as a political and military leader. Many of his marriages consolidated political alliances. All first five caliphs (leaders of the Islamic community) after Muhammad's death were Muhammad's fathers-in-law, as he had married their daughters - save Ali, the fourth caliph, who married Muhammad's daughter and was his son-in-law. The political function of marriage is evident throughout history.

Finally, his youngest wife, Aisha, has a special status in the prophetic biography. She is known to have been Muhammad's favourite wife, an important transmitter of legal reports about his conduct, and daughter of the first caliph Abu Bakr; but also as having married Muhammad when she was a child.

That this was unusual is evident from the emphasis that the Islamic sources place on her age; but the sources also clarify that the marriage was only consummated a few years later, when Aishah was probably a young teenager. Today, this seems unacceptable. However, the sources tell us that some of the widows that the Prophet married were in their later teens at the time of these marriages. This indicates that when they initially got married (to their first respective husbands) they were younger teenagers. That is, in seventh-century Arabia it was 'right' to marry young teenage girls.

Dr Peter Jones
Quaker, teacher and academic, Tasmania, Australia

Yes, Prophet Muhammad is recorded as having married twelve wives – not to mention having been given a number of concubines on top of that, a common practice back then. Today, political and religious leaders still give each other expensive gifts, but not quite like this. I can only explain the reason that this was regarded as acceptable back in the seventh century, although I am not sure what God thinks about it. Muhammad was first married when he was 25 and his wife, Khadija bint (daughter of) Khuwaylid, was 40. However other sources say she was 28 or 30, but all agree that her first two husbands had died. So she was a widow who actually proposed to him through a friend and by all accounts Khadija and Muhammad were happily married for 25 years. When she died Muhammad was bereft but at this point in his life, he was emerging as the leader of the umma or Muslim community in Medina where he had fled from Mecca in 622, after Khadija had died (619). For the next eight years, his community was engaged in battles with the people of Mecca and many of his Companions were killed. What we do know, is that almost all the women he married after he became the khalifa (caliph) or leader of the Muslim community, were older women who were the widows of those who had fallen in battle. Back then, there was no concept of a single woman, so marriage was the norm, and Muhammad married these women whose husbands had perished fighting for the survival of their community. The one exception that you refer to was his young child wife, Aisha, although there is some argument over how old she actually was when married to Muhammad. Her age varies in the hadith or records of the prophet's life, written down much later after he died. Some say she was married at six and the marriage was consummated when she was nine; other sources say she was a teenager. What we do know is that it was Aisha's father, Abu Bakr, who set up the marriage so that his daughter was allied to his political and religious leader, a common occurrence back in those days, and still practised in some countries today. You also have to remember that this was the seventh century and child marriages were very common back then, when sons and daughters had marriages arranged by their parents (often when very young) for political or diplomatic reasons – love and romance never entered into it!

43.

⁶What is the point of baptism?
Hitler was baptised so does this
mean he will go to heaven
(if this exists)?⁹

THE PHILOSOPHEr'S rePLY:

Baptism is central to Christianity. Jesus was baptised by John in the River Jordan and in Matthew's Gospel Jesus is recorded as saying that his followers should go out and baptise 'in the name of the Father, the Son and the Holy Spirit'. At Pentecost, after Jesus has risen from the dead, he is recorded as saying that he would send the Holy Spirit to be with them after he ascended into heaven. There are, of course, issues here – the doctrine of the Trinity took time to become established and whether Jesus actually said these words is a matter of debate (see Question 36). Nevertheless, Christians are clear that Jesus did say them and they represented a clear command.

Infant baptism (the baptism of babies) marks the wish by the parents for the child to be part of the Christian community and baptism is often performed as part of a normal Christian act of worship. Some Christian groups reject infant baptism and instead insist on adult baptism as they hold that a baby cannot make a decision to become part of the Christian community for themselves. Baptism should, therefore, wait until they are old enough to be able to make their own decision as to whether they wish to be baptised or not. In some Christian Churches, baptism as a baby is followed by 'Confirmation', which often takes place in the early teenage years and provides an opportunity for individuals to repeat for themselves the promises made on their behalf when they were a baby.

In answer to Question 48 the difference between the views of the British monk, Pelagius, and that of St Augustine of Hippo was explained. Pelagius rejected the idea of original sin (the idea that Adam and Eve sinned in the garden of Eden and, therefore, all their descendants are also in a state of sin). The view that baptism is essential to relieve people of the burden of original sin is, however, still held by most Christians even though most modern Christians consider the story of Adam and Eve to be only a story and not literally true. Increasingly some Christians hold that baptism is of more symbolic significance. In early Christianity, it was common for baptism to be postponed until people were near death as some considered that, at baptism, all past sins were forgiven but then sins committed after baptism were not. This, however, is not a common view today. Baptism, therefore, at least has a symbolic significance but many Christians would maintain that there is more to it than that – although exactly what the 'more' may be is not always clear.

We have no idea if there is an afterlife, and even if heaven and hell exist in some form, who will go where. To claim that baptism alone is enough to guarantee happiness in an afterlife does not seem to make rational sense and Pelagius' view seems far more persuasive to most people today. It is not, however, a view accepted by mainstream Christianity.

Professor Gavin D'Costa

Professor of Catholic Theology, University of Bristol

Baptism does two things. It cleanses you from original sin. It welcomes you into a family and community called Church, who seek to live together without sin. The first thing, cleansing, means that if you look around you will see a complex picture of what humans are like, but you will also see them as systematically destroying the environment, many seeking more money than they require, too often at the cost of others, and generally ruining lives – including their own. Being cleansed of Original Sin, as an adult or a child, means that you (and in the latter case as a child, your family), have come to a profound insight about the nature of reality. Humans were not created for destroying each other and our planet. We were created for love, joy, peace and caring about each other and the environment. Baptism says: yes we were created like this, we can live an alternative life, it is in fact who we are and who we can become – through help from outside of ourselves. The help is God – and the many folk who bring God to us. But note, this does not mean that you are automatically saved from that moment. Catholic Christians believe you must strive to live sinlessly – which is why the practice of 'Confession' is vital. Confession allows us to say, yes, screwed up again, but I know what I'm created for – and with your help (God and our friends), I want to set the ship right again!

Now to Hitler. Yes, Hitler was a baptised Catholic and from the evidence was a serious sinner. His actions represent a profound evil. He may also have had deeply troubling psychological disturbance from his very abusive father – as the analyst Alice Miller has argued. The latter point is simply to remind us that it is very difficult for us to be God – and 'judge' him. Does Hitler being baptised means he is in heaven?

Simple answer: no idea. One might sin relentlessly even after being baptised, so baptism is not an automatic entry ticket into heaven (if it exists – but we still need time to explore what 'heaven' might mean). But why do I say 'no idea' rather than yes, obviously he is in hell. Two reasons. The first I've outlined: I'm not God and cannot judge. This does not mean that we are freed from judgement on earth regarding issues of justice. Had Hitler not committed suicide, he would have stood trial at Nuremberg like the other Nazi war criminals. We do have responsibilities to judge good and evil regarding questions of justice. But that does not mean we have access to Hitler's conscience and heart. The second reason is also alluded to.

Sin requires someone to knowingly do wrong. In courts of law we have 'diminished responsibility' that might change a charge from 'murder' to 'manslaughter'. This kind of careful thinking must be applied when we consider Hitler. Read Alice Miller's account and ask yourself if you are confident Hitler is in hell (if it exists).

44.

‘If God is not an old man with
a white beard as the paintings
show then what is God?’

THE PHILOSOPHER'S REPLY:

There is great wisdom in Judaism and Islam which forbid any
representations of God. If God is the creator of the universe,
then any depiction of God is going to be nonsense – God
cannot be understood still less portrayed. The problem for
Christians is that Jesus is held to be both fully God and fully
human. If this is accepted, then pictures of the human Jesus are
actually pictures of God (as one of three aspects of the Trinity).
Once this step was taken (as it was in the ninth century) it was
an easy step to allow pictures to be painted of God – hence the
absurd pictures of an old man with a white beard sitting on a
cloud. Whatever God is (or is not), God is not that!

Far better to reject any portrayals at all and to accept
that God is beyond definition, beyond human understanding.
Sir David Attenborough refused to be called an atheist. He
said that when he looked down at an anthill that had its top
removed, he could see all the teeming activity of the ants but
they could not possibly comprehend him. How then could he,
a mere human, comprehend the God (if God exists) who is
held to be the creator and sustainer of all that is.

St Thomas Aquinas recognised this when he held

(following Aristotle, the great Islamic philosophers like Ibn Sina and Ibn Rush'd and the Jewish scholar Maimonides) that God is timeless and spaceless. If this is the case, then human beings (who are caught up in time and space) are incapable of understanding still less portraying God. There are basically two understandings of God:

1, God as timeless, spaceless, bodiless and absolutely unchanging. This God is beyond all human comprehension and is rightly described by the great theologian, Hans Küng, as 'Holy Mystery'.
2. God in time but without beginning or end, unchanging in character but the future is future to God. This is closer to the God portrayed in the Bible, but if God is within time and space then God would be part of the world of space/time and thus critics would say would be limited.

Neither model of God, therefore, is free from problems. Probably the best approach is to forbid all representations of God at all (as Islam and Judaism do) and to hold that God is beyond comprehension.

Professor Christopher Insole
Durham University and Australian Catholic University

The twentieth-century theologian Karl Rahner commented that it was worth thinking about the mere fact that the word 'God' exists.

If we do think about it, we notice several things. People from an early age use the word, and continue using it, even if they change their minds about what it means, or about whether they 'believe in God'. Also, the word God, or 'the divine', can be used in ways that are not monotheistic: for example, Einstein used the term 'God' to describe the harmony, order, and beauty in the universe; some of the romantic poets called human creativity divine, and contemporary pantheists *[believers that God and the universe are essentially one]*, including some modern pagans, speak about the divine when they regard the vitality and diversity of the natural world and the cosmos.

What might all these different uses of the word 'God' or 'the divine' have in common? The following is a hypothesis *[a suggested theory]*, which you can test for yourself, when coming across different uses of the word God.

If you are asked to 'think about your life', the first thing you might do is bring to mind everything that is most important to you: your hopes and plans, the people you love, perhaps a pet also, and the things in the world you would most like to do something about. Everything that comes to mind will seem like it *really matters*: and it does, because you, as a human being, are important. But, if you have ever tried thinking about the vastness of space, or of time, you might suddenly feel very small and insignificant: think of all the billions of years the earth existed without any sort of life, or all the billions of galaxies. The two ways of looking at yourself do not fit together very easily. In the first moment, you are the centre of a world. In the second way of looking at things, you are a tiny speck.

Where does God come in? Well, if you think that there is something in the universe, or beyond it, that offers the hope that these two ways of looking can come together and achieve an ultimate harmony and unity: perhaps, this is what is pointed to by the word 'God', or 'the divine'. The coming-together might not be possible yet, in this life, or it might be something achieved in our own mind. But, if it offers this hope of the 'coming together' of these ways of looking at our lives, we are inclined to call it 'divine' or 'God'.

Knowing what sort of thing the word 'God' does in our language is not the same as knowing exactly what, or who, God is. At least, though, we might have a better idea of what we are looking for, whether or not we think we find it. An old man with a beard would likely have the same perplexing questions about his own existence as us, and so might need to believe in God as well, and so could hardly be God himself.

Professor Gavin D'Costa

Professor of Catholic Theology, University of Bristol

Three answers.

One: You've not looked at enough paintings from non-Western cultures and even in the West there are different images!

Two: Some Christians are like many Jews and Muslims in refusing to depict God at all. This is on the basis of Exodus 33:20: 'Thou canst not see my face: for there shall no man see Me and live' (from the 'Old Testament') and John 1:18: 'No one has ever seen God, but the one and only Son, who is himself God.'

Three: The best depiction for God, for Christians who want to do representative art, is depicting Jesus Christ, who has seen God and is himself God, as St John says. Early Christians struggled with this question as they came out of a Jewish culture that forbade representation of that which could not be represented. Exodus 33:20 is clear. It should set the alarm bells going: no one can see God and live! The definition of idolatry is saying God is 'this' or 'that' because 'this' or 'that' is always part of creation and not the Creator. Even the capital 'C' for Creator acts as a kind of red light - indicating God is 'like', but also unlike, creators we know when we think of an artist or musician or a mother or father.

Okay, so why an old man with a white beard – like at the Sistine Chapel? Possible answers: this image may have derived from Zeus, the boss of the Greek gods. It also derives from the depiction of a patriarchal authority figure. Both are trying to say something about God: that God is powerful over all creation; God is the figure who looks after us. Of course, sadly, not everyone's 'dad' reaches those standards and some fall well short. There are real dangers in presenting God as a white bearded man. Dangers that your question brilliantly raises. Why not portray God as Mother? And why not a black mother, rather than a European? Both tradition and biblical language have pushed artists to keep faithful to 'Father', but actually, since God does not have arms and legs, let alone genitals, 'Father' finally is as much a metaphor as 'Mother'. Someone from whom all things derive, made us out of an overflow of love, and desiring friendship and joy for us – is an attempt to give a non-gendered description. *The Shack*, a novel by William P. Young, is well worth the read to unsettle our imaging of God. Every image presents problems, just as the absence of images does.

Why did I say Jesus is the best way to present images of God? Because that is what Christians claim! Who is God? Jesus is, but don't forget the two others: Father and Holy Spirit. Oh dear, that could easily lead to three gods! Make sure you are a skilful artist!

Dr Tommy Lynch
Reader in Political Theology, University of Chichester

The seventeenth-century Jewish philosopher Baruch Spinoza writes that God is everything. In his book *The Ethics*, he writes 'God, or Nature', rather than just 'God'. What exactly he means by this phrase is the source of endless debate!

THE 17TH CENTURY JEWISH PHILOSOPHER BARUCH SPINOZA WRITES THAT GOD IS EVERYTHING.

In my reading, he is making two points that can change the way we think about God. The first is that God is not a 'being' the way that you or I are. I think most people do not think God is really an old man with a white beard. It raises too many questions: Where is God? Does he have a left pinkie nail? How tall is he? Even so, it is common to think of God as a being. He is just the best being. He (because this God is often still masculine) is the being that existed before all the other beings: the creator and designer of everything that is. Spinoza's God is not 'a' being - God is being. That means God cannot be a He, She or They. God is everything. This removes the distance between us and God. God is not 'above' us in any sense. We cannot even say that God is 'in' us or 'in' nature because that would imply that 'we' or 'nature' are distinct from God.

The second way that this can change our view of God is by changing how we relate to other things (people, plants, animals, rocks, etc.). Take two people who are friends. In a traditional Christian concept of God, these two people are in a relationship with each other and with God. This forms a kind of relationship triangle which impacts how they treat each other.

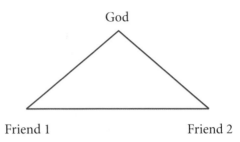

They might be kind to one another, for example, as a way of living out their relationship with God. In Spinoza's account, both friends are God. The grass where they sit and talk on a sunny afternoon is God (as is the sun itself). Even the friendship itself is divine. The triangle is gone and now there is something more like a web. The friends are not related to one another as two separate things, but different 'parts' of one thing.

Spinoza's idea of God may not work for everyone. In his own time, he was denounced by some as an atheist and by others as a pantheist (someone who believes everything is God - so pretty accurate!). His ideas do not sit easily in either the Jewish or Christian traditions, though some people have been inspired to incorporate his ideas into their understanding of those beliefs.

Still, I find something beautiful in Spinoza. I am not religious, but he captures something I have experienced. Sometimes, often early in the morning, I feel the wind, smell the grass, hear cows in the distance and see the sun starting to rise, and feel overwhelmed. In these moments, I feel less like a self—a 'me'—and more like I have dissolved into something big and beautiful. It is a 'something' where the differences between me, wind, grass, cow and sun have stopped mattering. I do not know what to call that 'something', but God seems like it could be the right word.

45.

'Isn't religion just a matter of being conditioned by your parents?'

THE PHILOSOPHER'S REPLY:

Philosophers always focus on key words to identify the issues! In the case of your question the key word is 'just'. It is almost impossible to argue against the view that children mostly adopt the religion of their parents. The evidence for this across the world is very strong. Shia Muslims tend to have Shia Muslim parents; Sunni Muslims, Sunni parents; Catholics, Catholic parents; Hindus, Hindu parents and so on. Some atheists such as Richard Dawkins use this as evidence to dismiss all religion as each religion tends to claim that it alone holds the truth and its view of God and what this entails happens to be the right one. Dawkins' argument is not, however, conclusive.

Much depends on whether one is going to hold to the view that only one religion is true and all the others are false. If this view is held, then the evidence that religious beliefs are passed on through families is exceptionally strong and the atheist's response may be convincing. This is, however, not necessarily the case. Religions have a great deal in common. They all teach the so-called Golden Rule – do unto others as you would have them do to you. They all warn of the dangers of focussing on wealth, money, fame, sex, possessions and similar preoccupations rather than on what really matters. They all maintain that every human life is incredibly important and that how one lives is highly significant. They (almost) all maintain a life after death and how one lives in this life will affect what happens in the next. There is, therefore, a great deal of common ground. Indeed if one measures the billions of people who have a religious outlook on life it probably accounts for 90 per cent of the world's population. It is largely in the affluent West (particularly in Europe, Australasia and New Zealand) that religion is marginalised.

It is fair, therefore, to recognise the dependence of most peoples' religious outlook on their parents although this is certainly not always the case and an increasing number of young people particularly in the West reject the beliefs of their parents. This dependence, however, does not invalidate the transcendent claims that unite religions more than divide them. This was a view that the philosopher John Hick came to at the end of his life. He was a Professor in Birmingham which is a multi-cultural city and he saw such goodness and saintliness in so many different religions that he preferred to speak to that which is ultimately Real (note the capital letter) to which all religions, at their best, point rather than using the word 'God'.

Dr Sue Price
Margaret Beaufort Institute

This is such an interesting question because I realise that in order to answer this question, I need to start not with religion but in a different place. From my research and involvement with children, the starting point for me is the innate spirituality *[something with which we are born and which remains with us]* that I see in all children. For me, that innate spirituality is that spark you both have deep inside of you that responds to and recognises the 'Something' that is outside of yourselves, the Something that is greater than you. Now, for many, the Something is called God, for many it is described as the Other, others don't have a name for it. For me, it is God, and that recognition and response to God is fostered, nurtured and grows through our relationships.

The relationships we have with ourselves, with our family, our friends and with nature all work towards nurturing our relationship with God and God's relationship with us. I suggest we desire to celebrate and support our relationship with God, and one way of doing that is through religious practice. Religion gives us a structure and a means of developing and growing our faith. Parents have a duty given to them through having you baptised to support and nurture your faith. One way they can do this is to introduce you to religion. So, I don't think religion is just a matter of being conditioned by your parents. I think it is their way of sharing what they think is best for you, to nourish and support you as your own spirituality forms. However, in the end, you will need to make your own decision about whether or not religion is what supports your faith and your spirituality. And don't be surprised if that decision keeps changing over time and with experience, that is all part of the wonderful richness of life.

DAVID GARRATT

Writer and Former Principal of Daramalan College, Canberra, Australia

For most of us, I think this is true. As we grow from childhood, we should be making choices for ourselves. Those of us who were christened at birth had no say in the commitment that came with the ceremony. Later on, in various religions, there is another ceremony, called confirmation in my religion of birth. This is meant to be when a person makes the commitment to their faith for themselves. It traditionally happened around the age of twelve. With my own children, I offered the choice of whether to join the 'automatic' confirmation in their school group or delay confirmation until they felt they were ready to make such a commitment. All of them chose to delay. All but one are no longer practicing the religion they grew up with, but they are living with strongly held values and have integrity, something which makes me proud. This is, if you like, another 'conditioning'. Our children are, by and large, reproducing the life values that we lived. Our example has helped to shape their character, their deeply held beliefs. That they do not go to church does not worry me. How they actually live their lives is much more important.

46.

‘In our school we are told how many Jews were tortured and killed by the Nazis. How can Jews believe in God if he allowed this to happen when he promised to look after them?’

THE PHILOSOPHER'S REPLY:

For some Jews, the issue you raised caused them to give up faith in God. At the heart of Judaism is a covenant relationship with God. A covenant is a binding promise between God and the Jews – God would always look after and protect the descendants of Abraham (God's chosen people) if they, in return, would keep his commandments.

Some Jews consider the terrible suffering brought about by the Nazis (the Shoah or Holocaust) to be God's punishment for them being unfaithful and disobedient. Others held that even in their utmost despair, God would bring good out of evil. Both answers are problematic.

Regarding the first point, whatever individual Jews may have failed to do in terms of obeying God's commands, to hold that God allowed the slaughter in the gas chambers of millions of babies, children, women and men and to know (if you were God) that the people you had promised to protect would die in the most horrendous conditions imaginable seems very hard (if not impossible) to justify.

On the second point, some Jews hold that God did bring good out of evil as the appalling events of the Shoah led to the creation of the State of Israel and the Jews once again having the homeland from which they were exiled for nearly 2000 years following the destruction of Jerusalem and it's Temple in 69ce. However, the creation of the State of Israel meant the people who have lived there for centuries (the Palestinians) largely being thrown out of their homes and driven into exile – an exile from which, 75 years later, they have still not returned.

The final answer that some Jews hold is that they cannot understand the ways of God and they will trust in God's promise even though it does not make sense to do so. Throughout history the people of Israel have survived. They have been persecuted, oppressed and every effort made to destroy them but, unlike all the other peoples of the ancient world, they alone have survived with their beliefs and trust in God largely maintained. This can be argued to be grounds for continuing to trust even though all the evidence seems to point in the other direction. This is hardly, however, a philosophic response but it represents the point where faith moves beyond reason. In other words, some will hold that in spite of all the apparent evidence to the contrary, in spite of the appalling reality of evil and suffering somehow, beyond all hope, good will triumph over evil and hope over despair.

Rabbi Professor Dan Cohn-Sherbok
University of Wales

Not surprisingly this question has vexed Jewish thinkers since the end of the Second World War. Some expressed overwhelming despair. The novelist Elie Wiesel, for example, explains in his autobiographical novel, *Night*, that religious doubts set in as he experienced the horrors of the Nazi regime. Describing scenes of terror, he portrayed the evolution of his religious protest. Unable to pray, Wiesel became the accuser. He simply refused to accept God's silence in the face of suffering and murder.

Arguing along similar lines, the founder of Humanistic Judaism, Rabbi Sherwin Wine maintained that Jews today must abandon their belief in a supernatural Deity. In his opinion, all theistic interpretations of God's involvement in history should be replaced by a naturalistic perspective. The world of reason, he states, has revealed that it has been a mistake for Jews to expect God to save them from disaster.

Other Jewish writers, however, continue to affirm their faith in God despite the horrors of the Holocaust. The Reform Jewish theologian Ignaz Maybaum, for example, in *The Face of God after Auschwitz*, argues that the Holocaust was part of God's providential plan *[God's long term, ultimate plan which humans cannot understand]*. According to Maybaum, it served as a means whereby the medieval institutions of Jewish life were eliminated in the Nazi onslaught against European Jewry. Hitler thus served as a divine instrument for the reconstruction of Jewish existence in the twentieth century. Jewish progress, therefore, is the direct result of this modern catastrophe.

Arguing along somewhat different lines, a number of Orthodox Jewish writers have attempted to make sense of the Holocaust in terms of God's aim for the Jewish nation. In his essay 'Manifestation *[demonstrations]* of Divine Providence in the Gloom of the Holocaust,' Hayyim Kanfo contends that God was present in the death camps. The horrors of the Nazi era were part of a divine process of redemption. The function of the Holocaust was to prepare the way for God's deliverance of the Jewish nation. In his opinion, the Holocaust constitutes the darkness before salvation. Out of agony and travail a new birth will take place. The Jewish people will go from destruction to national revival, from exile to redemption.

From these contrasting views it is clear that the Jewish community is deeply divided on how to make sense of the Holocaust. Yet, despite the clash of views, there is universal agreement that Jews must stand together in defending Jewry from future assault. Such a conviction is expressed most eloquently by the Jewish theologian Emil Fackenheim who maintained that God issued a 614th commandment out of the ashes of Auschwitz. Jews, he argued, are forbidden to hand Hitler a posthumous victory. 'They are commanded,' he wrote, 'to survive as Jews lest the Jewish people perish. They are commanded to remember the victims of Auschwitz lest their memory perish. They are forbidden to despair of man and his world, and to escape into either cynicism or otherworldliness, lest they cooperate in delivering the world over to the forces of Auschwitz. Finally, they are forbidden to despair of the God of Israel, lest Judaism perish.'

47.

‘At our school we performed a short version of *Macbeth* and we also acted out part of *Oliver Twist*. At first I thought these were true stories and only later discovered they were made up. Why don't we think that religious stories such as those about Jesus or other religious figures are also made up by their followers?
How can anyone actually know what they said (even if they existed)?’

THE PHILOSOPHER'S REPLY:

You are quite right. We cannot know what Jesus, Muhammad, Abraham, Moses, the Buddha, Guru Nanak or other great religious leaders actually said. The important word here is 'know'. The word 'know' implies certainty: as the head of

AT OUR SCHOOL WE PERFORMED
A SHORT VERSION OF MACBETH...

the Jesuit religious order said in a conversation with Pope Francis in 2019, 'There were no tape recorders at the time of Jesus'. While certain knowledge of what was taught and said is impossible, belief certainly is. Lack of proof is not the same as lack of truth. Religious people take seriously what is recorded in their sacred books. They see the sayings and teaching of the great religious leaders to have been confirmed and verified in terms of their wisdom and their ability to speak to succeeding generations down the centuries and seek (mostly or at least at times) to live their lives according to these teachings.

Often what a person is taught as a child by a parent will be carried down and its wisdom proved in practice as the child grows to be an adult. All religious leaders teach the importance of unconditional love and care for other human beings, for the need for compassion, justice, forgiveness and that life has a meaning and purpose. Almost invariably they proclaim a life after death and that how people live in this life will determine what happens after death. Jesus said that the whole of the wisdom of the Hebrew Scriptures could be summed up in two commands: 'You shall love the Lord your God with all your heart and soul and you shall love your neighbour as yourself'. No one can prove Jesus' actually said this but the whole of the Christian Gospels are totally consistent with this central message and, in a way, all the rest of Jesus' teaching are merely amplifications of this central theme. No proof is possible, but countless millions of people down the centuries have taken this seriously and sought to live by this message and, in so doing, have found a meaning, peace and purpose that they have found nowhere else. They would therefore claim that they are justified in their claim that they know Jesus' teaching to be true but, as in all religious matters, they could, of course, be mistaken.

James Roose-Evans
Author, theatre director and producer

First, we know from the historian Josephus that such a teacher as Jesus did exist. However, the Gospels (attributed to) Matthew, Mark and Luke are not biographical records or documentaries as we would expect today. Jesus had told his followers that he would return within the lifetime of his followers to judge the end of the world, and so it was in this expectation that his followers spent the next few years. Only when they realised the end of the world was not coming did they decide to try and collect as many of the sayings and deeds as people could remember so that there would be a record for those who came after them. This explains why the accounts vary, and some stories were probably invented. For instance, if Jesus did pray aloud in the Garden of Gethsemane who was there to hear him since his three companions were asleep? Clearly the writer here is trying to imagine the scene. Again, some of the stories of Jesus's miracles have been exaggerated for dramatic effect. For example, it is impossible for any human speaker, however skilled, even with a megaphone to communicate with five thousand people in an open space such as the desert! It would have been more likely two or three hundred. Again with the story of the feeding of the five thousand no one at that time would have travelled into the desert without a gourd of water and some dried fish in a leather pouch. So there was no magic conjuring trick by Jesus but by sharing what little he and his friends had set an example for everyone else to do the same, a much more important lesson! Also all the statements that Jesus had come to found a church and appointed Peter as its first head were later additions and inventions. What does come across to us is Jesus' emphasis upon loving God with all one's being and to love one's neighbour as one's self. And of course these two commands are found in all the great religions of the world. A religion is an attempt to understand the nature of the universe and of existence and to live in harmony with one another.

48.

‘Buddhism seems to be very sensible as it seems to focus more on how one lives and less on beliefs – why do beliefs matters so much? Surely how one lives is what is important?’

THE PHILOSOPHER'S REPLY:

This is a very perceptive question as its roots go back to the early Christian Church. In the early centuries of Christianity there were many differences of opinion and it took about 400 years for agreement to be reached. Two of the most important figures who dealt with your question were a monk from what is now Britain called Pelagius and one of the most important of the early Church figures – St Augustine of Hippo.

Pelagius agreed with you as he said that God would judge people by how they had lived – in other words by their deeds. He did not believe in 'original sin' – (the sin meant to have been inherited from what the stories in Genesis record as the first human beings – Adam and Eve). As we have seen, modern scholars consider that there are two separate stories in the first two chapters of the book of Genesis and they were written perhaps 400 years apart. In these stories, Adam and Eve disobeyed God and as a result were thrown out of a wonderful garden where there was no disease and no death. Evil, pain and death entered the world as a result of this event and every human being since then has inherited 'original sin' from these distant ancestors. Pelagius did not accept this story.

ALL SERIOUS THEOLOGIANS DO NOT THINK ADAM AND EVE WERE HISTORICAL FIGURES.

St Augustine, however, did accept the story. He did so because he wished to argue that Jesus had to be the saviour from sin – not only the wrong actions that we all commit but the original sin every human being has inherited from Adam and Eve (and which, of course, even babies suffered from). The only way to avoid being condemned as a result of both personal sin and original sin was to be baptised as a Christian and to receive God's gift of the Holy Spirit. This led Augustine to argue that only Catholic Christians could be saved: everyone else – non-Catholic Christians, babies, people who had never heard of Christianity – were condemned as they had not received the grace of God that came with baptism. Pelagius and his many followers refused to accept this. There was a battle between these ideas and eventually St Augustine won and Pelagius' position was declared to be a heresy (a heresy is a position that is rejected by the Catholic Church as unacceptable).

More recently, particularly after the important Second Vatican Council of the Catholic Church (1965-1968), the Church accepted that non-Christians could still be saved as Jesus died for all people and not just for Christians. The Church, however, still insisted on the importance of original sin and of people receiving God's grace in baptism. So whilst baptism has traditionally been seen as a release from sin, today it is more often seen as becoming a member of the Christian Church and significant not only because of this but because of Jesus' command to his followers that they should baptise people as he had been baptised by John the Baptist in the river Jordan. Buddhism focusses strongly on how life should be lived and this has consequences after death. It is, therefore, closely aligned with Pelagianism albeit without the Christian idea of God.

Professor Michael Barnes SJ

Professor of Interreligious Relations at the University of Roehampton

The Buddha uses a famous image to speak of the importance of the Dharma, the Buddhist teaching or truth. A man who is trying to escape from the terrors that oppress him finds himself on the edge of a broad river. The other side looks tranquil and more inviting but how is he to get there? He finds a makeshift raft and slowly paddles his way across. Once arrived at his goal, he puts the raft to one side and continues his journey. The Buddha himself comments: 'I have taught the Dharma compared to a raft, for the purpose of crossing over, not for the purpose of holding on.'

The parable seems straightforward enough and supports the view that Buddhism is itself thoroughly pragmatic. Make use of whatever practices or techniques or even beliefs as long as they are useful for a particular task. Once they have done the job, then discard them as you would a useful tool or instrument. In other words, the Dharma is there for a particular purpose and once that purpose has been achieved it ceases to have any importance.

This sounds plausible – and there is clearly something important in the pragmatic point of view. But it risks missing a more subtle point. The Dharma is a rich complex of material that includes both ethical and meditative practice as well as important teaching about the nature of the human person. There is more to the Dharma than a temporary and disposable raft. It is, to expand the metaphor, a complex of the two shores as well as the raft that enables the crossing from one to the other. Indeed, to separate them is to ignore one of the most profound aspects of the Dharma, the teaching of the interdependence of all things. The Dharma includes both the truth about the human condition, suffering and impermanence, the truth about the goal of human living, *Nirvana* or enlightenment, and the means to get there, the practices known as the Noble Eightfold Path. The parable is not telling us to abandon the Buddha's teaching when we achieve enlightenment. What we abandon is any provisional and inadequate understanding of the Dharma.

The principle can be applied beyond Buddhism. Christianity, for example, cannot be separated into beliefs about the nature of God that are revealed through the person of Christ and practices of prayer, ritual, sacraments, that give the beliefs a sort of practical superstructure. They are interdependent. What people believe is expressed in what people do, and their everyday actions – from praying the Eucharist to working for justice and peace – deepen faith and form wisdom and understanding. Any distinction between how one lives and what one believes needs careful scrutiny. They are intimately connected. Human beings are formed both by what they believe *and* how they live.

49.

'When people die their bodies
rot or are burnt. How can
there be a life after death if
this is the case as our brains
will no longer exist and so all
our memories will be gone?
Scientists have found no
evidence at all for the existence
of a separate soul.'

THE PHILOSOPHER'S REPLY:

There are two different ways of thinking of a human being:

DUALISM – this originated from Plato and considers that all human beings are made up from two distinct substances – soul and body. The soul is held to survive death and may or may not be reunited with a body.

MONISM – which rejects any idea of a separate soul and considers that matter can, eventually, provide a complete explanation of what it means to be human.

These two alternatives provided two different ways of looking at the possibility of life after death. If one is a dualist then one may hold that the soul survives death and, therefore, the body rotting or being burnt in no way undermines belief in survival of death. There is, however, no scientific evidence for this existence of a soul (although this does not rule out the possibility of the soul's existence).

If one is a monist then it is more difficult since, as your question makes clear, the body is completely destroyed. The philosopher John Hick argued at one time that God could create an identical replica of the person who died and this replica would then be her or him. The problem with this idea is that a replica is not the same as an individual: there could be more than one replica and to claim, for instance, that a replica of the Mona Lisa is the same as the original Mona Lisa is simply false.

If, however, one considers a caterpillar it could not conceivably imagine that it could become a butterfly. If there is a life after death there is no good reason to imagine that any attempt humans might imagine as to what it would be like would be anything like the original. The question of life after death remains open: Lack of proof is not necessarily the same as lack of Truth. I like the poem by Longfellow – in a way its message underpins many of your questions:

Life is real, life is earnest

1. Life is real, life is earnest,
    And the grave is not its goal;
    'Dust thou art, to dust returnest,'
    Was not spoken of the soul.

2. Not enjoyment, and not sorrow,
    Is our destined end or way;

But to act, that each tomorrow
Find us farther than today.

3. Lives of good men all remind us
    We can make our lives sublime;
    And, departing, leave behind us
    Footprints on the sands of time;

4. Footprints that perhaps another,
    Sailing o'er life's solemn main,
    Some forlorn and ship-wrecked brother,
    Seeing, shall take heart again.

5. Let us then be up and doing,
    Nor our onward course abate;
    Still achieving, still pursuing,
    Learn to labour and to wait.

The question of life after death remains open and, perhaps, is not that important. What matters is how one lives now and standing up for Justice, Truth, compassion, love and forgiveness are worthwhile ends in themselves – whatever may, or may not, happen after death.

RT REVD PETER CARNLEY AC
Former Primate of the Anglican Church of Australia

I think it may be helpful, in seeking an answer to this important question, to remember that a significant distinction may be made between the ideas of 'flesh' and 'body.'

The Early Church Fathers, for example, noting that Paul had said that 'flesh and blood cannot inherit the Kingdom of God'

(1 Cor. 15:50), often distinguished the body from the material particles of flesh and blood of which it was composed. The flesh is obviously changing as a person grows and matures, but the same body remains, making it recognizably and identifiably the same. This already squares with our own daily experience. Every time we visit a barber some of our bodily cells fall to the floor and are swept away, at other times we lose tonsils, appendix, a thyroid, and so on. Our eyebrows are said to be replaced every 60 days or so. Indeed, the molecular or cellular components of our bodies are constantly being replaced.

Some Early Christian Church Fathers used the analogy of a river to illustrate this: just as the drops of water that constitute a river pass by and eventually disappear into the ocean but the actual, identifiable, river remains, so it is with the fleshly particles that make up the human body. This changing fluidity or plasticity of human bodies is something that is in accord with the science of modern quantum physics.

Only comparatively recently, I have come to learn that Hebrew has no word for 'body'. It has a word for 'flesh' and so the Psalmist can say 'My flesh will rest in hope' (Psalm 16:9). But St Paul in the Hellenistic world, who in expressing the Christian hope in Greek, was furnished with the word soma/body, and so came up with the phrase 'the resurrection of the body' while drawing a contrast between being raised with Christ and 'remaining in the flesh' in this material world.

Admittedly, some early Christian Creeds, particularly in the West, spoke of the 'resurrection of the flesh', whereas in the East the preferred language was 'the resurrection of the Dead' or the 'resurrection of the Body.' Eventually, the West began to conform with the Eastern usage. In our Prayer Book, for example, Archbishop Cranmer changed the Apostles Creed at Mattins and Evensong from 'resurrection of the flesh' to 'resurrection of the body.'

The importance of Christian belief in 'the resurrection of the body', as distinct from 'the resurrection of the flesh,' is that the flesh may pass away, 'ashes to ashes, dust to dust', but God's gift of an identifiable new life beyond death in the resurrection of the body is yet another thing. After all, heaven is not an extension of the material world, neither a place nor a state located in some other region of the universe. Rather, heaven is essentially a relationship with God, the very relationship we enjoy in reconciled unity with God in the communion of the Holy Spirit that is known in faith already in this world. In hope we interpret our knowing of it in the concrete experience of our earthly lives in a promissory way, as the down-payment or guarantee of more to come.

Hence, with St Paul, while 'flesh and blood cannot inherit the Kingdom of God,' Christians confidently affirm our belief in 'the resurrection of the body.'

HOW DO I MAKE SENSE OF LIVING A RELIGIOUS LIFE?

50.

‘Jesus told the story of Dives and Lazarus yet many people who go to Church are wealthy compared to people who are very poor so how can they call themselves Christians?’

THE PHILOSOPHER'S REPLY:

Much depends on definitions – particularly what it means to be a Christian. If being a Christian means being baptised, believing certain things and going to church regularly or occasionally then there is no contradiction in being incredibly wealthy and a Christian. Rupert Murdoch is a Catholic and a billionaire – he even has a knighthood given by the Pope (he is a knight of the Papal Order of St Gregory). Many incredibly wealthy people go to Church so if going to Church makes a person a Christian then there is no contradiction.

Your question, however, goes beyond this. It is not only in the story of Dives and Lazarus that great wealth and ignoring the needs of the poor and vulnerable is criticised. Jesus constantly warned of the dangers of wealth. Indeed, given the Christian Churches and their emphasis on sexual morality over the centuries when Jesus hardly talked about this at all and their equally ignoring all his teaching about the danger of wealth it would seem that many Churches consider Christianity to be about Church attendance.

Very recently, Pope Francis (the leader of the Catholic Church which is by far the largest Christian organisation with over a billion members) has switched the debate. He has constantly called for Christians to live simply and to safeguard and to care for the environment. At the end of 2021 he spoke to an assembly of Church dignitaries in Rome and called for them to show humility and to adopt a simple lifestyle. Some senior Catholics dislike him for saying these and similar things but it would seem that if Jesus' teaching is taken at face value, then he has a perfectly fair point. I suspect he would agree with your question. So, as always in philosophy, much depends on definitions of what you consider a Christian to be. It seems to me that it is an extraordinarily large claim for anyone to make: The philosopher Nietzsche said that there was only one true Christian – and he died on the cross. Maybe this is taking it a bit far, but one can see his point.

Gerard Windsor
Author and literary critic

The rich get a sticky press in the Bible. We all know that 'it is harder for a camel to pass through the eye of a needle than for a rich man to enter the kingdom of heaven'. Yet the Bible is full of rich people and lots of them come up smelling roses. Solomon 'arrayed in all his glory' is the paragon of wisdom, and for all his faults he is, like his father King David, one of the goodies. Jesus was proud to claim his descent from David. In the New Testament Jesus is buried in a tomb owned by Joseph of Arimathea, obviously a rich man, owning his own tomb, able to finance all the spices and oils for the dead body. And Joseph was rewarded *[according to legend]* by being given the Holy Grail, the cup used at the Last Supper, and bringing it with him to England, to Glastonbury.

Never having been rich myself, I suspect there are certain dangers in living in a bubble of wealth. Maybe you're cocooned from a poorer world, maybe it's harder to feel empathy, maybe all your material goods suffocate any self-reflection, any thinking of what life involves other than accumulation. As Fagin sings in the musical *Oliver!*, 'In this life one thing counts, in the bank large amounts'. But I know wealthy people who have avoided these traps. And some poorish people who don't rate as angels.

Obviously it's what you do with your money that's the decisive factor. When Jesus told us the criteria by which people would be accepted or rejected into eternal life, he didn't specify being rich as a prohibiting sin. Rather it was for not feeding the hungry, or not tending the sick, or not visiting those in prison, that you got the chop.

Dives is not condemned for being rich. It's his treatment of the beggar, Lazarus, that does for him. Dives and Lazarus is one of those wonderfully simple, wonderfully moving stories that we find in the New Testament. And, like the others, it's the odd detail that sets the seal on them. In Moissac, in the Tarn-et-Garonne department of southern France, in the portico of the twelfth-century abbey, there are sculptures. Thrilling as they all are, my favourite is a depiction of the story of Dives and Lazarus. Dives and his cronies are feasting. Lazarus is on the floor, under the table (actually outside the gate in the Gospel but there's limited space on the sculpture wall). But there's an angel flying over him, and in the next scene we have a huge, bearded man cradling, it seems, a baby. In fact this is Lazarus 'in the bosom of Abraham' where he's been carried by the angel, and where Dives is refused entry. The whole tableau is both crude and magnificent, and my *pièce de résistance* is the inclusion of the authentic Gospel detail - two large dogs licking the sores on Lazarus who lies ignored and rejected under Dives' table. The rich man who ignores dogs licking someone's sores is definitely a goner.

51.

'The early Christians shared everything and no one was in need yet many Christians are incredibly wealthy and the poor starve. How does this make any sense?'

THE PHILOSOPHER'S REPLY:

In Jesus' time there was no social security, no free health care, no unemployment pay and no pensions. In many countries this is still the case today but, at least in Europe, Canada, Australia and New Zealand there is an effective social care system paid for by taxes. It could be argued, therefore, that the requirement for the rich to look after the poor is partly catered for by the taxes paid by the rich. This does, however, seem to miss the point of Jesus' teaching. He seemed not only to criticise those who did not do enough for the poor but, more than this, he criticised wealth itself. Many people have argued that money does not bring happiness – certainly if one is desperately poor and cannot afford housing, food, heating, education or basic health care then a modest amount of money can transform peoples' lives. Many, however, have a far higher standard of living and accumulation of possessions than that which is necessary for a comfortable life.

So there are two points. First, wealth above what is needed at a fairly basic level can distract people from what is really important in life such as kindness, compassion, empathy, the beauty of the natural world and the courage to stand for what is good and true: so wealth by itself can lead people away from a truly virtuous life. Once wealth and possessions dominate one will always want the bigger car, the better mobile phone, the bigger house, etc. Secondly, if all human beings are regarded as having rights merely by being human, then a failure to care for the refugee; those living in poverty; those in prison or homeless; those who are lonely or bereaved or distressed is a moral failure.

Peter Singer is a brilliant atheist philosopher who writes about this at length and lives it out in his own life, giving more than 20 per cent of his income away and seeking to persuade people that they have a moral duty to care and to live simply. In this sense, his life is probably closer to the life Jesus would have wanted than those of many so-called Christians today. In fact in terms of Social Justice teaching, Pope Francis and the atheist Peter Singer have much in common although they differ totally on the sanctity of human life (c.f. Question 13).

SISTER GEMMA SIMMONDS CJ, PH.D.
Director of the Religious Life Institute, Cambridge

It makes no sense at all, in Christian terms, and you are entirely right to challenge this! The Acts of the Apostles is the chronicle of the emerging Christian community as it became an identifiable group with characteristics of its own, separate from the Judaism from which it sprang. This idea of the early Christians sharing everything comes from Acts 2:42-47 and is repeated in Acts 4:32-37. We get an idealised picture of the early community living in perfect unity, praying together and following wholeheartedly the teachings of Jesus, especially what he said about giving up one's wealth and possessions to care for the poor (Luke 18:18-25). 'All who believed were together and had all things in common; they would sell their possessions and goods and distribute the proceeds to all, as any had need.'

This sounds wonderfully inspiring and some people, like St Barnabas, actually did this (Acts 4:36-37). But even in Jesus' own lifetime we hear his followers questioning his teaching about giving away money and possessions (Luke 18:24-30). The desire to cling on to possessions and security and the fear of going without runs very deep in people. Learning to let go of these deep drives towards money, security, success and power is a lifetime's job, even if we long to be free of them. As the church grew, young people wanting to live a radical Christian life went out into the desert to live in total simplicity, giving up their status and wealth. This is the beginning of what would become religious orders, whose members actually take lifetime vows to give up their possessions. Most of them (think of people like Francis of Assisi or Mother Teresa) really mean it and do dedicate their lives to the poor. But sadly, the history of religious life also shows people losing sight of these ideals and becoming rich, pampered and powerful, despite their promises.

Acts 5:1-11 tells the story of a couple who try to have it both ways and cheat God by lying about how much they have given away. The community interprets their sudden death as God's punishment. That may not be literally true, but it suggests that they took Jesus' teaching on wealth and the need for charity and justice very seriously. Later on, quarrels within the community emerge about the distribution of funds (Acts 6:1-2). This tells us that this human drive towards possessions persists, even when people are trying to live up to high ideals. This doesn't mean that having ideals is pointless, or that people who fail completely to live up to them are hypocrites. But it does tell us that following Jesus' teaching on charity and justice requires a daily 'Yes' from us in ways both big and small.

52.

‘St Francis called for people to live simply and Pope Francis has done the same, but few people take any notice in the wealthy world. Are they still Christians if they are selfish and spend their money on themselves and possessions?’

THE PHILOSOPHER'S REPLY:

Philosophers can be infuriating at times and they often say, 'it all depends what you mean by ...' and that is the case here. The question is what it means to be a Christian (the same point I made in answer to Question 49).

Søren Kierkegaard was probably (at least according to Ludwig Wittgenstein who was possibly the most influential philosopher of the twentieth century) the greatest philosopher of the nineteenth century and a saint. He profoundly tried to live a Christian life but never dared call himself a Christian as he thought this was too big a claim to make. For Kierkegaard, being a Christian meant centring one's whole life on God and putting everything else into second place. He renounced until he died marriage to a woman with whom he was head over heels in love, he renounced any idea of a family and was tortured by his own inadequacy, yet was absolutely sure of the love of God. He was highly cynical about priests with their long robes and concern for their financial wellbeing and was even more critical of the Lutheran Church of Denmark, yet few people devoted more of their lives to work at what it means to be a Christian.

There are going to be many answers to the question of what being a Christian means. For some it just means going to Church each week, for others it just means a vague idea that they were brought up as a Christian and therefore when asked what their religion is will reply 'Christian'. Kierkegaard's point was that if one places the Christianity found in most Churches on a Sunday against the Christianity set out by Jesus, the tremendous differences will immediately be obvious. He argued that to say one is a Christian simply because your parents made love and, after you were born, a priest sprinkled some water on your head and said a few words is nonsense – it is far, far more challenging than this.

Wealth alone would not rule out someone being a Christian but much depends on what one does with this wealth. How much is devoted to one's own pleasures and needs (whatever these may be considered to be) and how much is devoted to improving the lot of those who are poor, ill, in prison or vulnerable. Francis of Assisi, Pope Francis, the Buddha, the Sikh Guru Nanak and most great religious leaders would call for people to live simply and to devote ourselves to the good of those in need. If someone claims to be a Christian and does not do this, it might be argued their claim is largely devoid of content.

Dr Anna Abram

Principal, Margaret Beaufort College, Cambridge

Saint Francis lived in the twelfth century in an era of big economic and societal changes that required him to adapt from the feudal and agricultural world to the new urban and commercial world. He came from a wealthy family who ran a business. Yet the lifestyle and values of his privileged circumstances didn't satisfy him. For him, simplicity that he found at the heart of the Christian message was the key principle for life. His commitment to simplicity was linked to his passion for building peace and seeing beauty in the natural world and dignity in everyone. He was keen to create harmony amidst turmoil, poverty and illnesses, especially leprosy (an infectious disease which carried stigma and segregation) which was very common then. He was known for sharing any possessions he had.

Money and possessions are not bad in themselves. The problem is not that people have goods and are wealthy. The problem occurs when we accumulate more than we need and take no notice of those around us who have very little. Often (though not always) wealth is created at the expense of the poor and the natural world. But, if people are not exploited, are paid justly for their work, and are willing to share, wealth can be a good thing. For example, during the COVID-19 pandemic, it turned out that the key workers such as nurses, staff in care homes, people who clean public spaces or deliver food receive small salaries while others who work in banks or businesses can earn even 100 times more than those working in care homes. It is these inequalities, driven often by greed and stigma of physical work (seeing it as less important than other jobs) that damage our communities. The pandemic has also put the spotlight on some wealthy members of our society who became known for sharing their wealth and living simple lives. They sponsored meals for the key workers, delivered food for the vulnerable, paid for hotel accommodation of the homeless, and financed projects to advance the wellbeing of others. These examples suggest that being wealthy is not a bad thing as long as material goods are not seen as goals in themselves but rather as means to do good.

Of course, we need more than individual acts of sharing by wealthy. Those acts, however, matter too even if ultimately we need fair systems that provide the same opportunities (education, healthcare, employment, etc) for everyone.

A core concern for Saint Francis of Assisi wasn't the existence of wealth. It was the existence of poverty at the expense of the poor and a lack of solidarity with the poor. The same concerns, eight hundred years later, are on the agenda of Pope Francis. In his encyclical (a formal and important document) called *On Care for Our Common Home* (known by its Italian name *Laudato Si'* which comes from 'Canticle of the Creatures' by St Francis), Pope Francis reminds us that excessive interest in material goods can be a distraction from things that are more important such as friendship, love of nature, and harmony in the world. Pope Francis recognises that living a simple life is a challenge for everyone because human beings have a propensity to get attached to possessions and ignore the needs of others and of the natural world. Therefore, he encourages us to rethink our relationship to the nature and see it as our 'common' world. This world is to be shared and looked after and not to be possessed and exploited.

Pope Francis wants everyone to think of the needs of other people, especially the poor, and to find value in commitment to simplicity. So, when we fancy a new pair of expensive trainers or another mobile phone, we should ask ourselves: 'Do I really need this?' or 'Why do I need it'? St Francis didn't judge those who had possessions, but he was clear that wealth is for sharing. He even saw thieves who prey on others, and sometimes suffer hunger, as his brothers. We might say that this was a rather extreme attitude and not many people can be as saintly as he was. We can still learn from him and Pope Francis that the heart of the matter about wealth is a proper consideration of the other. The 'other' here means – another human being such as my sibling, friend or a stranger. The 'other' also means the natural environment (our common home) through which we are always connected to each other. Both the rich and the poor, for St Francis and Pope Francis, are the children of God.

53.

'When Jesus was being nailed
to the Cross he asked God to
forgive the soldiers as they
did not know what they were
doing. How then can God send
anyone to hell as most people
who do wrong also don't know
what they are doing?'

THE PHILOSOPHER'S REPLY:

Of all the questions you have asked, this may be the hardest
and it is certainly one that I have never thought about. Jesus in
asking God to forgive those who are nailing him to the Cross
is clearly showing, in an extreme way, the forgiveness that he
demands that all his followers should show to anyone who
wrongs them. The prayer that Jesus taught his followers says:

'Forgive us our sins, as we forgive those who sin against
us.'

This is incredibly challenging and many Christians ignore
it. Jesus is saying that God will forgive the wrongs committed
by his followers in the same way that his followers forgive the
wrongs committed against them. This is hard to recognise,
still less to live up to. In the passage you quote, however, the

Roman soldiers are not asking forgiveness – instead Jesus says they do not know what they are doing. Clearly Christians take this to mean that the soldiers do not recognise that they are killing God's son (which is the central Christian claim). However, Jesus is not saying, 'They do not know who they are crucifying.' Your question is, therefore, very challenging because you are right – many people do not know what they are doing.

It is easy to wonder whether the worst people we can imagine really knew what they were doing. Even Hitler was trying to restore his country after what he saw as the humiliation of the First World War. The Jews were a convenient scapegoat. Hitler was loyal to his friends, loved the children of friends of his as well as animals. Did he really know and appreciate what he was doing? Everyone assumes so – but the same assumption could be made of the soldiers who crucified and mocked Jesus.

It is, perhaps, possible to hope that Jesus was right and God will forgive everyone who does not know what they are doing but Jesus does not seem to indicate that this is the case (consider the story of Dives and Lazarus or the parable of the talents). It is possible, of course, to simply ignore this saying and to argue it is hyperbole or something that applies only in the particular situation in question, but there is nothing in the text to indicate this.

CANON THE LADY AILSA NEWBY
Canon of Ripon Cathedral

There are two key understandings at the heart of Christianity. The first is that God loves us and wants us to love him in return but he does not force us to love him: we are free to do as we choose. This is sometimes called our 'free will'. When we choose to love God and do what is right, God rejoices: it is just what God most wants. The second key understanding is that God is incredibly merciful and, if we do wrong, if we do not love God but are sorry, we are immediately forgiven. No ifs or buts, just forgiven, all put right.

The soldiers at the cross I imagine did not know the enormity of what they were doing: killing the Son of God. As you say, it is true of many people who do wrong. Sometimes, too, we don't realise what we are doing is wrong until afterwards. Then there is forgiveness, if we admit our fault when we realise it.

I'd say God does not 'send' anyone to hell. We have free will – the chance to decide – and the chance to say sorry when we realise we've done wrong. Although it may be true to say many people do not know they have done wrong, I believe that, when we leave this life we will have such a complete experience of the presence of God that we will have complete understanding, both of God and of ourselves and our own failures. Then we will know exactly where we have gone wrong and have the chance to say sorry.

So, if we do not make that choice to say sorry, when we meet God face to face, we choose wrong for ourselves. Then you could say that we will be choosing to send ourselves to hell. It is not what God wants. He wants us to say sorry, to love him and to spend eternity in his loving presence. But, humans always have that choice: to say no to God. And that could end in hell. For this reason, hell is sometimes described as simply the absence of God. Maybe, just maybe, no one in history has ever refused to say sorry when faced with God. Hell might just be empty.

As for those soldiers, it was Jesus' compassionate kindness, always caring for others, that made him pray as he did. I'd hope that the soldiers, even if they did not realise what they had done wrong then or later in life, when they came face to face with God in death, would have realised, been sorry and are now enjoying eternal life in God's presence.

THE REVD DR RICHARD LEONARD SJ
Parish Priest, North Sydney, Australia

Some people see Jesus' ability to forgive the soldiers from the cross as a sign that He was God ... because what human could be so forgiving? As the poet Alexander Pope said, 'to err is human, to forgive, divine'. I don't see it like that. Jesus does not forgive the soldiers himself, but asks His Father to forgive them. This is odd because previously Jesus' many healings and exorcisms *[casting out devils or demons]* show that He had the authority to forgive sins himself and because Jesus asks God to do something, apparently not knowing if He will, and excuses the soldiers saying 'they know not what they do' as if God didn't know what they knew.

Why then does Jesus ask God to forgive the soldiers? If Jesus was fully human and so born in sin (Psalm 51), then He would have forgiven the soldiers himself because in the Lord's Prayer He taught the disciples to pray 'forgive us our sins as we forgive those who sin against us' and in His parable of the unmerciful servant (Matthew 18) He taught that God's mercy depends on ours. If Jesus needed God's forgiveness then it would be conditional on His ability to love His enemies and pray for those who persecuted Him (Matthew 5). It follows that Jesus asking God to forgive the soldiers shows either that Jesus did not need God's forgiveness or that He did not want it.

In the film *Dead Man Walking,* the mother of the murderer showed what human love is. As a mother she can't believe the truth that her son was a murderer, she then makes excuses for her son, then blames herself, then implicates herself in trying to protect him. When Jesus says 'forgive them Father, they know not what they do' he shows that He loves His enemies in a very human way, making excuses for them even as he knows the excuse isn't true, making excuses for himself in forgiving them when He knows that doing so offends justice. So, when Jesus says 'forgive them father, they know not what they do' he shows not that He is fully God, but that He is fully human. He is asking God to do something that he knows God can't and won't do for a reason that He knows is not true. Jesus is so human that, like you, He can't accept that God's goodness lies in sending most people to Hell, to the extent that he put his whole being between them and it, as that mother put herself between her murderer-son and the Law.

Of course, Christians believe that Jesus, while fully human, was also fully God... but that is another question!

54.

> ⁶If you just have to obey God
> could you not be just like a
> robot and not be free at all?⁹

THE PHILOSOPHER'S REPLY:

I am not sure this question makes sense! The question says 'If you just have to obey God' – if this means that we are programmed robots who have no choice then, of course, we would not be free at all. If, however, the question means 'If you are meant to obey God' then this leaves entirely open the possibility of free will. The great monotheistic religions (Judaism, Christianity and Islam) all maintain that living a life centred on God is the only real way in which human fulfilment is to be found, but this in no way undermines human freedom. Many choose to ignore God and to live simply for their own pleasure – this is their free choice. Understood, therefore, in this second way, there is no tension between the call to centre one's life on God and human free will to decide whether to do so or not.

PROFESSOR C. STEPHEN EVANS
Baylor University, Waco

The answer to this question depends on what is meant by 'have to obey.' If having to obey God means that one is forced to obey, either by God's interfering with a human person's will or by coercing that will, then obeying God would indeed infringe on human freedom. In the former case, in which God interferes with a person's will, a person would indeed be like a robot with no free will. In the second case a person would be more like a slave, obeying out of fear.

However, God would find no delight in having people 'obey' him in such ways. Amazing as it sounds, God wants humans to be his friends, and friendship cannot be coerced but must be voluntary. God has therefore chosen not to create robots who would always do what he wills, nor slaves who obey out of fear, but has given us the gift of freedom.

I believe, therefore, that 'have to' should be understood differently, as meaning 'ought to'. We ought to obey God because he has proper authority, just as we ought to obey a human ruler who has proper legal authority. In fact we have more reasons to obey God than any human authority because God is perfectly good and loving and only wills our good. We should want to be his friends because that is where our deepest happiness lies. The truth is we do not have to obey God in the first sense of 'have to', and it is sadly true that we often do not obey him, even though if we fully understood and willed our own good, we would choose to do this.